PERPETUAL TRANSFORMATION

PRACTICAL TOOLS, INSPIRATION AND BEST PRACTICE
TO CONSTANTLY TRANSFORM YOUR WORLD

Library of Congress Cataloging-in-Publication Data has been applied for.

ISBN:
978-1-62825-756-4 (Paperback)
978-1-62825-757-1 (eBook)

Published by:
Project Management Institute, Inc.
18 Campus Boulevard, Ste. 150
Newtown Square, Pennsylvania 19073-3299 USA
Phone: +1 610 356 4600
Email: customercare@pmi.org
Internet: PMI.org

Design by www.jebensdesign.co.uk

PERPETUAL TRANSFORMATION

PRACTICAL TOOLS, INSPIRATION AND BEST PRACTICE TO CONSTANTLY TRANSFORM YOUR WORLD

www.brightline.org
www.thinkers50.com

First published in the USA 2022

Contents

Foreword

Pursuing a transformation agenda is no longer optional; it is essential for business survival. Nor is it a six-week program or an initiative; it is a state of mind, a philosophy, a part of organizational DNA. Transformation is unending.

Over the last several decades, leaders have talked extensively about change — especially as the pace of disruption has accelerated like never before with the dawn of the Digital Era. Barely a week passes now without another (virtual) conference on achieving change, the publication of a freshly minted book on the subject, the introduction of a new business school program on the topic, or an announcement of another corporation dedicating itself to change.

But how to actually implement change? Many organizations turn to outside experts to help them turn all of the "change" talk into reality.

These experts often come equipped with the latest thinking and models which explain how change can be achieved. These models are often brilliantly captured and communicated. They are then unleashed; change programs and initiatives rolled-out across teams, divisions, departments, sometimes entire organizations.

For all the sound and fury surrounding change, however, virtually every piece of research on the subject suggests that organizations still remain very poor at turning the change into reality. Too many businesses are seeing their change programs deliver disappointing results, ground to a halt, miss targets, drift into oblivion, or get replaced by newer and shinier versions.

In the twenty-first century, change has been increasingly reconfigured as transformation. While change suggests subtle, targeted improvements, transformation is more far reaching, ambitious and challenging.

And in truth, it never quite ends. Transformation isn't a distant shore or destination, but a continuous journey.

This new language of transformation isn't decorative. It reflects a realization that tinkering at the edges of organizational behavior and performance is not enough.

Just think of the challenges we have all faced in the last decade: a global financial meltdown. A pandemic of historic proportions. And, the relentless and unstoppable forward progress of technology reinventing companies, markets and all corners of the world for today and tomorrow.

So, welcome to the new reality which is powerfully mapped out in the selection of insights captured in *Perpetual Transformation*.

As the articles gathered together here make clear, perpetual transformation is difficult, challenging, endless, stretching and involves rewriting the rule book. None of that makes it less necessary.

Though it might appear daunting, perpetual transformation actually confirms the realities which business legends have always acknowledged: now is the time to transform, not tomorrow. The choice is there for every manager in every organization. I hope that *Perpetual Transformation* provides the inspiration they need — and their organizations demand in order to continue to succeed.

Michael DePrisco
Chief Operating Officer at Project Management Institute

Digital transformation for teams that are not digital-first, yet

RAHUL AVASTHY

1

D igital transformation helps you think value, not profit. Yes, it's important to focus on creating a new digital business that increases customer willingness to pay more for a product or a service, because if you can find a way to improve a product or service, you can increase willingness to pay. This is where you start thinking of new business models, and hence there is a lot of attention toward the commercial and revenue-generating teams; however, it's imperative to understand that support teams provide valuable "moments that matter" in the critical journey of the digital transformation of an enterprise.

The need for support teams to plan, understand consumer behaviors that they value, and employ creative innovation is more critical now than ever. Many support teams deliver service in a spectrum, and this spectrum ranges from full service to self-service. In between, there are varying degrees of collaborative service, where the organization and users share the responsibilities of the service. Seeing service with this perspective will allow you to think of digital as something that helps organizations share accountability along the spectrum.

A significant change is already in motion, driven by the acceleration of digitization; various functions like operations, HR, administration, accounting, credit control, legal, communication, finance, and other support functions within an enterprise, face the risk of being diminished to an efficiency-first support role. Digital transformation for support functions, if implemented without the right strategy, may (wait, may? let me not be polite — will) magnify the revenue-generating organization's flaw within an enterprise.

The increase in volatility and complexity, accompanied by uncertainty and ambiguity, also known as VUCA, makes the decision-making process complex. Simultaneously, noncommercial/support functions must give guidance to the business based on transparent and mutually agreed criteria with clear accountability. Many support functions that may not get digital-first priority as commercial/revenue-generating organizations within an enterprise have complex processes, unearthed deep data stories and may make their outcomes slower as dependencies grow further.

So, what to do?

For support teams looking at digital transformation, having a defined vision, clarity of value contribution, and reimagined self-perception, numerous support functions can help reimagine the opportunities digitalization offers to develop into a digital enabler that shapes the entire organization's digital ecosystem. Eventually they have to enable revenue generation or increase willingness to pay for the customers.

Leverage automation: Among other tactics, these teams should consider being partially automated, leading to more efficient processes and ultimately leaner, outcome-focused organizations within an enterprise. Digital transformation needs a range of skills, meaning there is a place for everyone involved. Generalists will be valued contributors to simplify the processes, while specialists are required to implement the new techniques. It's a misconception that digital reduces the job roles within an industry. Look at Google translate as a service; ever since machines have started leading translations, jobs for translators as a category have increased year over year.

Invest in DDDN — data-driven decision networks: For example, HR, legal or finance functions may combine operational and financial data (big data if matured or advanced analytics, to begin with) and utilize AA (advanced analytics) and ML (machine learning) to enhance business agility while acting as a collaborative service provider to an enterprise organization within an enterprise. This will lead to more engagement and a new perception of adviser and partner to business units, and not just a controller or touchpoint enabler while guiding them in their decision-making process.

It's critical as traditional role models face a trade-off between efficiency and value proposition to the business, as increases in output are linked directly to the rise in input (resources). Digitalization can help resolve the target conflict between pure and cost-efficient versus comprehensive and value-contributing at high costs. How do you do that? Cost-efficiency can be triggered by automation, which helps to redesign and streamline processes with RPA/ robotic process automation technologies, especially for transactional processes.

Relevance to the business can be described as data-driven insights. Today's restriction may be neither the availability of data nor the integrated technology infrastructure to handle large data volumes. The critical requirement and challenge is to evaluate those data in a structured, efficient, and targeted method. This is where the data analytics and advanced analytics role come into action.

Summing up:

1: Scale-up planning
- Set target
- Formulate hypothesis
- Align strategic initiatives and what not to do
- Strategy — look forward and reason back: use data
- Allocate resources, rethink funding model as more agile
- Establish milestones

2: Translate vision
- Clarify vision
- Gain consensus

3: Communicate
- Goals and progress
- Change management
- New value proposition
- KPI measures
- Best practices / next practices

4: Cyclic iteration
- Onboarding
- Agile delivery
- Evidence-led decisions
- Outcome vs. output
- Measure and controls.

If you are in the driving seat, think about how you can empower and enable support functions that don't get digital-first priority as commercial/revenue-generating organizations within an enterprise to tackle the real business problems. As teams become comfortable with failing fast, learning along the way is expected and should not deter further progress.

Perspectives can change a lot; reimagine an organization's view as a connected collection of collaborative service providers to internal or external clients. The first step to build such a modular organization is to chart out the critical path, simplify processes and move out steps off the critical path. Know what not to do. Look forward and reason back.

Believe and you can fly.

About the author
Rahul Avasthy is based in Chicago and leads digital transformation and experience at Abbott Laboratories.

Beyond digital transformation: What's next?

DIDIER C. L. BONNET

2

How often have you heard senior executives stating that "digital transformation is not a project but a never-ending journey?" At one level, it makes sense. After all, there will always be another wave of technological innovation that will have the potential to improve an organization's performance even further. But, strictly speaking, when you look up the definition of *journey* in the Oxford dictionary, it describes it as "The act of traveling from one place to another," strongly implying that there is indeed a destination at the end of the journey.[1]

So, who's right and who's wrong? Are you destined to endlessly move your organizations through perpetual cycles of digital transformation? Or is there indeed a destination, an end-game, to your digital transformation efforts?

Our research shows that the end game of digital transformation might be a bit more nuanced than those diverging questions would imply.[2]

It's clear that the relentless pace of technology innovation will not slow anytime soon. Innovators and engineers will continue to do a great job of bringing us ever more sophisticated technologies. That's great news. Moreover, we believe that the pace of technological innovation will probably accelerate, providing us with endless opportunities to improve the way we operate and manage every corner of our organizations. Technological heaven, then?

Yes — but for some, it can also be a rather scary thought. Many executives know how hard it is to succeed at digital transformation, and many others have already failed. We've seen many large firms struggle through the first two phases of digital transformation. First, digitizing their existing operations and second struggling even more to use digital technologies to transform the way they relate to customers, improve operational performance and equip employees to work more effectively. After a decade of digitally transforming our organizations, you would have thought this would have become mere table stakes. But the game has moved on. Today, we're at the cusp of a third stage in digital transformation. A stage that requires firms to shift to new business models, fully connect and automate their operations and augment employees' capabilities through human-machine collaborations.

Yet again, we are hitting a traditional brick wall when it comes to the relationship between technology and organizations. That is, the progress and performance of digital technology might improve exponentially, but the speed of transformation of our organizations and institutions is anything but. So, what can be done to close that gap? Do we assume this is just the way the world is? For the sake of a bright digital future for our organizations, we shouldn't.

Changing our mindset for what's next

There's no question that digital technology has provided a seismic shift in the performance of our organizations, in individuals and entire societies. But is digital transformation a perpetual phenomenon in today's corporate management? At some point, everything should become digital, right? Hence, one of the most common questions I hear from executives about digital transformation is *what's next?*

Many executives, academics and consultants are looking for the holy grail of the post-digital world or for a "third shift" from the industrial age to a digital age to some other age. The common answer to the *what's next* question is all too often expressed through another wave of technological prowess. Quantum computing, cognitive computing, distributed ledgers or ever more "intelligent" artificial intelligence algorithms. Problem is, most analysts, or self-proclaimed futurists, revert back to technology as the central framing mechanism for the future of digital transformation. And, as much as technology progress is critical, we believe this is wrong.

When we look at economic history, we find that every technological revolution has been followed by organizational transformation. With steam power, work shifted from home to factories, with significant scale economies. With the electric motor, energy sources could be decentralized enabling autonomous and more efficient ways to manufacture goods. Frederick Taylor then laid the principles for scientific management by optimizing and standardizing work. So, why are our organizations today still structured and continue to work and operate roughly in the same way as they did in the 1960s?

The coming years will witness digitally-driven changes in the business world that make everything we've experienced in the early days of digital transformation look like the opening act. And, beyond the prowess of technological development, it is organizational and work adaptation that will represent the biggest change for our businesses and our people. We're not there yet by any stretch of the imagination. But what's clear is that it is *organizational and managerial innovation* that is today the missing link to extracting the maximum productivity from the digital revolution. It won't happen overnight, but it is the key to transitioning to *what's next*.

The digital organization destination

The holy grail will indeed be the process of graduating from digital transformation to a digital business. More specifically, the ability for corporations to make the "act" of digital transformation second nature.

What we've learned in the last decade is that both the main accelerators and the main hurdles of digital transformation are not about technology but about leadership, people, organization structures, incentives, culture or internal politics. It's the softer (but the harder, i.e. more difficult) side of the equation that will propel organizations to the ultimate stage of digital transformation, that of *becoming a digital organization*.

When digital transformation becomes business-as-usual for your organization, for your people and your customers, you'll be there. In other words, it will become transparent in the way you run your organization, manage your people or leverage new waves of technological innovation. It does not mean that you will cease to work with physical assets or people, it means that your business and operating models will be built on a foundation layer of digital processes and data. A digital bank may still have branches, but behind the scenes you will find a set of digitally-enabled operating procedures that ensure the customer experience will be consistent across all channels.

It's about a new organizational DNA anchored around digital mindsets, practices, capabilities and behaviours. We have not yet found the exact organizational and work structures that will allow companies to fully leverage and profit from the digital revolution. There are, unfortunately, no silver bullets to becoming a digital organization. It's hard work, and will be a long-cycle transformation. But luckily, we have a few pointers toward the destination.

On becoming a digital organization[3]

Powerful digital technologies, ubiquitous data and advanced algorithms offer new strategic choices for products, services and business models. But at the same time, these technologies also present new organizational choices for designing, coordinating and managing people and work. The narrative on digital transformation, to date, has placed relatively little attention on the organizational challenge of executing our chosen digital strategies.

Business leaders get bombarded with advice such as "act like a start-up," "be agile and adaptive" or "Uberize yourself." But how useful is this advice when you run a large complex organization? Although we have a better understanding of the characteristics of a truly digital business, leadership is about developing the version that works for your organization. Your culture, leadership style, organizational structure, complexity and globality matter in how you craft your path to a digital organization. Most large firms are not known for being nimble and agile. So how can these organizations develop the corporate agility required to become a digital organization and compete effectively and sustainably?

Previous research shows that becoming a digital organization is about reaching a sustained organizational ability to rapidly adapt and self-organize to deliver value through emerging technologies.[4] It requires rethinking how you organize as well as how you operate in new and productive ways. It also requires an adaptive workforce. This isn't easy. Becoming a digital organization remains an aspiration for most firms. Our research shows that most organizations are in a state of transition. Even among traditional firms that are mature in the execution of their digital transformation, only seven percent are close to becoming a true digital business.[5] There's no off-the-shelf answer, but there is a blueprint.

The cadre of companies that have reached the status of digital organization exhibit a number of common characteristics — a new digital DNA: A "digital mindset"; a digitally-savvy and technologically augmented workforce; data-driven decision making; and an ability to self-organize and orchestrate work at scale. A tall order indeed. (Figure 1).

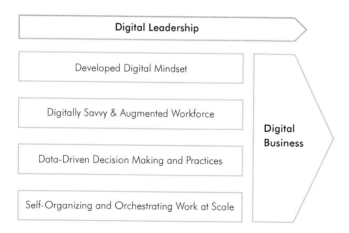

Figure 1: Becoming a Digital Business

This destination is more a marathon than a sprint and, at times, can be uncomfortable. It requires tenacity and resilience. Foremost, it requires strong leadership to steer the course and keep the organization focused on the end goal. But it's worth the effort. Digital organizations are able to adapt to narrow windows of opportunity or respond to significant external events quickly. In other words, digital transformation, as an orchestrated process, will no longer be required.

A Developed Digital Mindset: Digital transformation has made business transformation and technology intrinsically linked. A positive and proactive attitude toward digital possibilities is particularly important. In digital organizations, an instinctive *"Digital* Mindset" is evident in how people throughout the firm explore digital solutions before traditional process-based ones, systematically using digital tools and data analytics. It's about challenging the status-quo and constantly looking at technology as a way to remove traditional operational and competitive constraints. It favors using technology and a zero-based approach to problem solving, automating tasks to the extent possible, and encouraging digital experimentation and innovation. Challenging existing industry norms, excelling at open innovation, being hyperaware of the external environment, and becoming more agile as an organization are some of the ways to get to a digital mindset.

Richard Fairbank, Capital One CEO, noted: "Digital is who we are and how we do business. We need to make digital how we do business not only with our customers, but also how we operate the company."[6] As employees experience and publicize successes with a "Digital Mindset" approach, positive attitudes cascade and spread through the larger organization.

Digitally Savvy and Augmented Workforces: Raising the digital IQ and developing key skills in an organization have been key challenges in digital transformation. They become a must-have when operating as a digital organization. And it's not a one-off. The need for continuous learning becomes greater, not smaller. Reinventing how we enable continuous learning, at scale, for our employees is paramount — and a major transformation for our existing HR and learning functions. Digital organizations also demonstrate an elevated organizational capability to use tools and data to dynamically deploy and reconfigure both human work and capital resources at speed.

Then there is automation. As a rule, digital organizations default to automating core processes, especially repetitive and unproductive tasks. But the bulk of existing jobs are not displaced, they are augmented. Automation takes away much of the tasks that used to bog down workflows, leaving humans to focus on more fulfilling and relevant tasks. Human-machine collaboration becomes greater than the sum of the parts. Robin Bordoli, CEO of machine learning company, Figure Eight, described the potential as follows: "It's not about machines replacing humans, but machines augmenting humans. Humans and machines have different relative strengths and weaknesses, and it's about the combination of these that will allow human intents and business process to scale 10X, 100X, and beyond that in the coming years."[7] For instance, in radiology, computer-based algorithms have increased the productivity of diagnosing simple cases but, more importantly, are assisting medical professionals to concentrate on the most complex diagnoses. A better outcome.

Data-Driven Decision Making: Oftentimes in digital transformations, people are enthusiastic about big data and the power of analytics to support strategic decisions. Truth is, most of us believe strongly in our own powers of intuition. And this is not a bad thing — human judgment still matters in digital organizations. Jeff Bezos, founder and CEO of Amazon, commented that there are two types of decisions: "There are decisions that can be made by analysis. These are the best kind of decisions. They are fact-based decisions that overrule the hierarchy. Unfortunately, there's this whole other set of decisions you can't boil down to a math problem."[8] So, business judgment will not completely disappear in the digital organization (probably a good thing), but the primary default mindset is clearly fact-based — from customer to operational to people decisions. It even extends to the way you innovate and conduct experiments. Of course, to become data-driven in your decision making, you need access to quality data timely, accurate and complete.

Good data aids employees in improving internal business operations and responding effectively to customer demands. To truly leverage the investment in digitization, organizations must use their accumulated data in systematic analyses that drive important strategic decisions, as well as to monitor and refine internal processes. Data enables digital organizations to be more tightly orchestrated and controlled than ever before. And, paradoxically, this is a prerequisite to more employee autonomy. As employees and management realize the benefits of data-driven outcomes, they use fact-based approaches more consistently, creating a virtuous cycle.

Self-organizing and Orchestrating Work at Scale: Organizational design is not a perfect science. Over time, whichever way you organize, silos will reappear. Of course, the first trick is to organize so as not to entrench silos along reporting lines or functional domains. But whichever way, digital initiatives, to be successful, will cut through your organizational construct. Digital organizations display an ability for team and work fluidity. It is based on *collaborative learning*. Teamwork and partnering to solve problems without regard to discipline, geography, ownership or other traditional parameters, and ensuring insights and solutions move rapidly and readily across boundaries. Organizational leaders help by setting clear goals, encouraging boundary-spanning collaboration, providing liberal access to relevant information, and then trusting their employees to bring their best expertise to bear for each challenge. Is this just about agile programs? No. It goes way beyond agile processes and tools. In digital organizations, agility and nimbleness are embedded in the DNA and the mindset of how work is carried out and how people come together, interact and collaborate. With tighter synchronization and control through data and analytics, digital organizations can confidently give more autonomy to their people. It's the shift to higher levels of *self-organization*.

Chinese company Haier, the world's largest appliance maker, took digital transformation a step further by innovating its organizational model to mimic the architecture of the internet. The company is organized around 200 customer-facing micro-enterprises and over 3,500 service and support micro-enterprises. It took Haier the best part of 10 years to redesign its core workflows and change workforce mindsets to make it work. But it has paid off. Chairman and CEO, Zhang Ruimin, explains what drives the success of micro-enterprises: "Successful micro-enterprises have three characteristics. First, they are very entrepreneurial and very good at identifying, developing and seizing new market opportunities, so that they can develop those markets and seize the opportunities. Secondly, they are very well self-organized. They are also very open to inviting people from outside their organization to join them in their research and development. The third characteristic is that these successful micro-enterprises are self-driven and very motivated. They are always looking for the next opportunity to grow."[9]

Reaching the level of a digital organization has two important corollaries. First, digital organizations have porous boundaries, with an ability to access and source talent externally quickly and efficiently be they machine learning experts from a top university, software solution innovators from start-ups, or coders from the gig economy. Second, internally, digital organizations are able to deploy resources and expertise flexibly where customer or operational opportunities exist, beyond organizational boundaries, P/Ls or budget cycles. When such a level is reached, workforce engagement and intrapreneurship become outcomes.

How far is your business from becoming a digital organization? Ask yourself the following questions:

- How far do you think your organization is from having a digital mindset?
- How digitally savvy is your workforce? Are you thinking about how automation can augment the value-added of work within your organization?
- Do you have the data and the mindset needed to be data-driven in your decision making?
- What is the ability of your workforce to self-organize across traditional boundaries?

If by now you're feeling depressed by the size of the challenge you're facing, don't be. You're not alone. Most organizations are transitioning towards a digital organization, but few are there yet. What's important is the ability to gauge progress. There are clear signals that can help you know whether your organization is moving closer. For instance, when digital solutions come first in problem-solving, or when collaboration and sharing takes over from managerial coordination, there is no more need for separate digital governance.

What's important is the aspiration and the drive to steer your organization ever closer to the edge of the digital organization. It's about leadership. However, leaders cannot mandate the development of values and norms such as collaboration, self-organization, and fact-based decision making. But they can cultivate the conditions that encourage new mindsets and practices through, for instance, role modeling and encouraging cross-silo collaboration or practicing and requiring data-driven decision making. And sometimes, it needs a level of organizational surgery to make it work.

So, is there an end to the perpetual need to transform organizations? Most likely not. Business transformation is a leadership and managerial endeavor that will remain important in a constantly changing competitive world. But is there a destination for your digital transformation efforts? Most definitely yes. Working at becoming a digital business will allow you to close the gap between the relentless progress of digital technology and the ability of your organization to profit from these new technology-enabled ways of working. It's about *organizational and managerial innovations* and it has become as important, and probably even more, for digital transformation success than a sole focus on technology innovation.

About the author

Didier Bonnet is Affiliate Professor of Strategy and Digital Transformation at IMD. Professor Bonnet's research, teaching and consulting interests focus on digital economics, digital strategy, disruptive innovation and the process of large-scale digital transformation for global corporations. He is the co-author of *Leading Digital: Turning Technology into business Transformation* (HBR Press, 2014) and *Hacking Digital: Best Practices to Implement and Accelerate your Business Transformation* (McGraw Hill, 2021).

Footnotes

1 https://www.lexico.com/definition/journey

2 M. Wade, D. Bonnet, T. Yokoi & A. Obwegeser, *Hacking Digital: Best Practices to Implement and Accelerate Your Business Transformation* (McGraw Hill, 2021).

3 Adapted from M. Wade, D. Bonnet, T. Yokoi & A. Obwegeser, *Hacking Digital: Best Practices to Implement and Accelerate Your Business Transformation* (McGraw Hill, 2021).

4 D. Soule, G. Westerman, D. Bonnet & A. Puram, "Becoming a Digital Organization: The Journey to Digital Dexterity", SSRN 2697688, 2016.

5 D. Bonnet et al, "Organizing for Digital: Why Digital Dexterity Matters", Capgemini Consulting research paper, 2015.

6 Capital One Q4 2013 earnings call.

7 https://www.salesforce.com/video/1718054/

8 B. Girard, *The Google Way: How One Company is Revolutionizing Management as We Know it* (No Starch Press, 2009).

9 "For Haier's Zhang Ruimin, Success Means Creating the Future", Knowledge@Wharton Podcast, 2018.

Putting employees and customers at the heart of transformation

TIFFANI BOVA

3

What conversations are taking place in your boardroom about customer experience (CX) and employee experience (EX)?

As organizations look to build back better post-COVID, the focus has typically been around the need to streamline operations, adjust product and service offerings, restore profitability and rebuild partner and supplier relationships.

But the pandemic has also acted as a catalyst for a seismic shift in what customers expect from the organizations they buy from — and in what employees expect from the organizations they work for.

If companies are to remain competitive, they will need to find ways to balance the demand for high quality, fast, digitally enabled services with the increasing pressure from consumers for a responsible, sustainable approach to business.

In the era of 'the great resignation,' where there is fierce competition for the best talent from a dwindling pool, employers will also need to rethink the way they treat their people, moving issues like employee well-being, skills development and flexible working much higher up the agenda.

A strategic approach to CX and EX will be fundamental to organizations efforts to navigate the tides of perpetual transformation — and the two are inextricably linked. Happy employees who feel their organization cares about them will perform better and are more likely to give customers the quality experience they are looking for.

So what is the best way to get the experience equation right?

A symbiotic relationship

The link between customer experience and sales is well established. But recent research from *Forbes Insight and Salesforce* suggests that the situation is more nuanced. In its 2020 report 'The Experience Equation: How Happy Employees and Customers Accelerate Growth,' it suggests that CX and EX enjoy an intricate relationship, where one depends on the other to gain maximum results.[10]

The study is based on publicly available customer and employee satisfaction data, together with interviews with 300 US-based senior executives from companies with $20million plus annual revenues.

One of the key findings is that revenue growth is linked to high EX, regardless of the priority placed on CX. Companies with both high EX and CX, however, see almost double the revenue growth [1.8x] as those who rank low on both. For a billion dollar brand, that is a $40 million dollar positive impact.

Seventy percent of executives agreed that improved EX leads directly to improved CX, which in turn leads to rapid revenue growth. The message is clear: if a company wants to drive expansion, it needs to begin by paying attention to the experience it is offering its employees.

Getting the equation right has benefits beyond improved profits. Organizations adopting this approach also find that employees are better aligned with organizational goals, more open to technological change and more likely to display innovative and collaborative behaviors. Overall, this adds up to greater organizational capacity for change and transformation.

What's interesting to note, however, is that the equation doesn't work as a virtuous circle, where revenue growth automatically leads to high EX and CX.

Revenue growth doesn't necessarily make employees happier. As business booms, for example, employees may find themselves having to work harder and harder to meet customer demands. If the right resources, training and processes are not in place to support them, they will soon become tired and frustrated.

Organizational design

What implications do these findings have for organizational design? The report suggests that creating a value proposition that benefits all stakeholders is key. There is no point, for instance, in creating great customer experiences if they are not aligned to the employee experience.

A common mistake organizations make is emphasizing one part of the equation at the expense of the other. The survey found, for example, that despite recognition of the interdependent nature of the two, 65 percent of executives said CX was likely to be a more important strategic objective than EX over the next three years.

But there are ways to improve both EX and CX concurrently. Just under half of the leaders interviewed for the survey agreed, for example, that getting employees fully invested in the success of the company by structuring incentives around CX and EX would improve both. Creating teams that combine CX and EX skills is another way to achieve alignment.

When it comes to improving CX and EX, however, organizations often find themselves facing some obstacles internally — and what the research highlights is that CX and EX executives differ significantly in their views about what these are.

CX executives point to a lack of the senior management vision needed to drive change, while EX executives suggest the problem centers around employee resistance to cultural transformation.

Opinions about how to overcome these challenges is divided, but what's clear is that close coordination within leadership teams is crucial if operational strategy is going to focus around the task of enhancing both EX and CX.

The role of leadership

The study suggests there are some lessons to be learned about how leaders in smaller companies create an environment where both CX and EX sit happily alongside each other.

Average Glassdoor employee ratings tend to be higher at smaller, high growth companies than at larger, more mature firms.

At times of rapid growth, employee engagement in these smaller firms often increases despite the pressure, thanks to empathetic leadership and a strong team ethos. In high-growth situations where this strong leadership is absent, chaos can ensue, damaging both CX and EX.

The key to success is to create an environment where individual initiative is rewarded and employees can blossom along with the company.

Four steps to success

The study highlights four steps companies can take to succeed in the new landscape of always-on transformation.

1. **Align the company with strong leadership and vision:** If organizations want to drive change and achieve sustainable growth, they need a clearly articulated senior management vision. The C-suite needs to instill a sense of common purpose and focus on developing an organizational culture that aligns both CX and EX to these shared goals.

2. **Align operations and IT strategy to focus on CX:** Nearly half of the executives surveyed said the pandemic is leading to a fundamental reassessment of how to enhance customer experience. There is likely to be greater strategic emphasis on CX rather than on EX over the next three years, but this prioritization might hamper the organization's ability to grow rapidly. Finding the right balance is key, and technical solutions can help companies improve both CX and EX.

3. **Incentivize cross-functional teams to enhance both CX and EX:** The biggest organizational obstacle to improving CX and EX is when a company emphasizes one more than the other, or has conflicting priorities. To overcome this, employees need to understand exactly how

their roles play a part in enhancing customer and employee experiences. There is also a need for greater collaboration between those working in EX- and CX-critical roles.

4. **Invest in technologies to measure CX and EX:** The average organization has 900 applications, only 28 per cent of which are currently integrated.[11] It's vital that companies stop operating in silos and making investments that are not necessarily crucial to employees' day-to-day work. Having systems that will yield valuable data to help executives understand the variables driving both customer and employee sentiment is key.

About the author

Tiffani Bova is the global growth evangelist at Salesforce and the author of the *Wall Street Journal* bestselling book *GROWTH IQ: Get Smarter About the Choices that Will Make or Break Your Business*. She is a Thinkers50 ranked thinker.

Footnotes

10   "The Experience Equation: How happy employers and customers accelerate growth", 2020 Forbes Insights, sponsored by Salesforce.

11   https://www.mulesoft.com/lp/reports/connectivity-benchmark

Thriving in a persistent transformation context

EDIVANDRO CARLOS CONFORTO
AND JULIANA MENDES

Almost two years after the first case of COVID-19, and a lot has changed in our lives and in many organizations across the globe. What had seemed impossible, like asking all employees to work from home, in some organizations became a reality in just a few weeks. What made such a radical shift possible so quickly? To a certain degree, it was those who were best prepared in terms of an agile operating model, technology adoption and processes, that were able to quickly mitigate some of the negative impact caused by the pandemic restrictions.

For example, at Accenture China, we distributed over 80,000 desktop computers within a week to the homes of staff.[12] Thanks to a clear plan, the company was able to make this shift quickly and fully embrace a work-from-home operating model.

Many organizations had to review their strategies to overcome the crisis. The difference between those organizations that will thrive after the pandemic and those that will struggle lies in the organization's capability to deal with a persistent transformation mode.

Fast forward one year and discussions have begun about returning to the office. Another massive change lies ahead of us. What will it look like? What should we expect in terms of productivity? What is the right balance between home and office working? In just two years, organizations have had to "transform" themselves more than once.

In this article, we share recommendations to help leaders prepare their organizations for the state of persistent transformation.

There are several elements to this:

Build a hybrid environment

First, organizations need to build a hybrid environment. The pandemic forced many firms to break their traditional boundaries to allow people to work from home. Now, having seen the positive results, many firms are rethinking the purpose of working at the office. Research suggests people's expectations are changing about what is coming and what we might expect when we are all able to return to work safely.

In one recent study, for instance, eight out of ten workers from different industries said a hybrid model would be optimal.[13] Unfortunately, the reality is that most HR policies are based on in-person work prior to COVID-19, and 90 percent of the global workforce was onsite. When it comes to going back to regular work, people seem to want a different approach (see Figure 1, A and B).

A) What drives people to want to be remote?

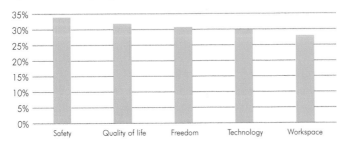

B) What drives people to want to be onsite?

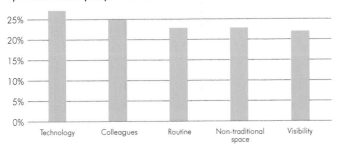

Figure 1. People's perception about what they want at the office and remote. Source: Accenture Research — The future of work: Productive anywhere, 2021. (% of people who strongly agree, sample size 9,326 respondents).

Looking at the top priorities listed in the figures above, it is clear that one of the main challenges for those who want to work remotely as well as those who are willing to work from the office, is how to create a 'hybrid environment' where people can enjoy the benefits of both work models.

One strategy is to develop 'adaptive spaces' to foster connections, help teams collaborate, innovate and experiment, combined with a digital approach that will allow workers do their job from anywhere.[14]

From a management perspective, hybrid management models have emerged to help organizations cope with innovation and dynamism, while at the same time balancing discipline and predictability. Leaders are recognizing the importance of combining different management approaches to deal with the diversity and complexity of their strategic initiatives. With the limitations and restrictions caused by the pandemic, teams had to find new ways of interacting and collaborating to keep productivity at the same level as before.

But how can organizations raise the maturity level of their workforce to sustain and even ramp up productivity? Intelligent working models have come to light to help balance the adoption of technology, methods, practices, and processes enabled by a great cultural change. On top of that, discussions about incentives have also emerged. More than ever, it is necessary to review the metrics, compensation, benefits, and the whole incentive model to give people a strong foundation to align their purpose with the company's goals and objectives. The goal of adopting a hybrid management model is to combine what works best for the business needs, leveraging different frameworks and tools and, most importantly, align the business needs and challenges with people's purpose and expectations.[15]

Here are some recommendations to build a hybrid environment:

- Design your own strategy for the post-pandemic context. Consider different scenarios and manage all potential risks to avoid surprises and keep operations running smoothly while transitioning to this new normal. Initiate a transition period to new workspaces as well as roles.
- Consider implementing an intelligent operating model to align with the needs of a new scenario. Don't simply copy, but use frameworks and tools as a reference (e.g., agile, adaptive, iterative), and make sure you define some boundaries to indicate which type of activities can be executed remotely and which should be completed in person. Be mindful about the differences in the incentive model for each scenario.
- Define clear business objectives, to allow the business vision and strategy to permeate from top to bottom to increase the transparency and discretionary decision making at all levels of the value chain, allowing autonomy and decentralization of decisions. An intelligent model will help leaders to build autonomy with accountability.
- Make sure the organization provides the technology required for the hybrid operating model. Building people's technology literacy will help workers deliver the best result no matter where they are. Focus on building the right level of maturity so teams will choose the best approach to do their job.
- Leadership must be transparent about the challenges and genuinely listen to their team, who typically knows where the friction and challenges are. This journey will require leaders who are open to learning and able to adjust as they go along.

Make agility pervasive

It is undeniable that COVID-19 forced leaders to think differently about the changes needed in their organizations — from the changes in the workforce to the urgency of dealing with climate change. What we have seen is a rush toward digital transformation and innovation.

Some leaders tried to recover the years they did not act toward transforming their organizations and the underinvestment in technology, organizational modernization and new ways of working. Most organizations today need business agility capabilities to be able to consistently anticipate, adapt and accelerate to respond to change. Several studies have reported the business benefits of adopting agility at all levels, including better financial performance, long term and sustainable growth, innovation, resiliency, flexibility, customer satisfaction, people culture and behavior.

In 2015, research from MIT revealed evidence about the use of agile practices to develop agility capabilities across different areas and in different industry sectors.[16] From the product level up to the ecosystem level, it is essential to develop agility capabilities to cope with changes in people behavior, product requirements, operations objectives and goals, and business strategies.

To make agility pervasive, leaders need to understand the essence of agility which can be summarized in three main aspects.[17] First, agility has different and multiple dimensions (see Table 1 as an example). Second, agility is a capability, not a method: just adopting a framework or method will not automatically turn your organization into an agile powerhouse. Third, agility is dependent on multiple factors, which, depending on the business context, may include culture, incentives, organizational structure, governance, budgeting strategy, team configuration, access to technology, and so on. Simply copying frameworks from successful cases may not work for your organization.

Dimension	Examples	Focus
Organization	HR, Marketing, Finance, Technology, or a Business Unit	To respond to business environment challenges and opportunities
Process or Operation	Manufacturing, Supply Chain	To respond to changes in production demands, flow (including supply chain)
Product or Project	One product line or a project	To respond to changes in user requirements

Table 1. Dimensions of Agility. Adapted from Conforto, et al., 2016.6 [17]

Regardless of the dimension of agility, those organizations that have mastered agility are organized around value chains. And this is a big change in the way a business is structured, especially for those organizations that are more traditionally organized around business functions.

Although some organizations have reaped the benefits of agility, many others still struggle to make agility a strategic topic and adopt it on a scaled level. Due to the pandemic, organizations have accelerated the adoption of agility capability, but not all have mastered it. Just one third of the organizations studied, according to recent report, have already adopted an agile workforce strategy at scale.[18]

So, if you are the leader of a large enterprise, there are a few questions to help you understand where you are on this journey. Is agility on your priority list? Are you discussing agility with your leadership consistently? Are you adopting agility at scale (from the product level up to the strategic level)? Do you consider agility as an enabler to deliverables or results?

To make your agility capability pervasive, we recommend the following steps:

- Agility is driven by common principles: define a set of common principles that will guide the behavior of teams, and teams of teams: for example, collaboration, autonomy, continuous learning, transparency, purpose driven, etc. It is essential to adopt intelligent operating models that promote collaboration and experimentation. Encourage efficient, top-down, bottom-up communication.
- Connect with strategy: objectives should be driven by strategic goals and measured by customer value. Some competencies combined with agile methods are useful in the search for quick responses regarding potential business benefits. Another key success factor is to adopt the lean portfolio management approach to balance investment between business as usual and innovation, in addition to implementing techniques for dynamic budgeting. It allows companies to make faster and more assertive decisions to escalate or pivot in short learning cycles.
- Scaled by design (not only by IT capability): adopt a top-down and bottom-up approach. Think holistically and include all areas of the organization in the agile transformation initiative. To implement, start small and scale fast. Focusing on continuous learning, experimentation and a data-driven approach will provide the best transformation ROI.

Speed is critical, as are consistency and clear benefits. Setting up a Business Agility Center of Excellence may help align key stakeholders around common purpose and goals.

- Connect with the business ecosystem: with the democratization of data, experience-led transactions, changes in financial market and regulations around the globe, the balance of the business ecosystem is changing. This trend opens new possibilities for collaboration. As a result, new incentives outside the corporation's borders become increasingly powerful. It is essential to understand the business ecosystem and encourage new ideas to remain competitive and make the right partnerships.
- Measure continuously: if you don't measure you cannot improve or, worse, you cannot prove benefits. Adopt data analytics from the portfolio level down to the product development level. Digitally-enabled metrics, which are evidence-based, will help leaders make better investments and understand the causal relationship between business results and agility capability.

Leverage technology as a service

Technology adoption is one of the factors that enables a hybrid environment, as it supports and enhances business agility development and performance. One way to look at technology now is from a business disruption standpoint. Every business depends on technology or will be a technology business in the near future. Therefore, it is crucial to understand how technology is driving transformation in your business sector.

To put this into perspective, a study of 10,000 companies across 18 industry sectors and over 10 million datapoints indicated the level of disruption in some sectors, many of those impacted by technology advancement. To some extent, banking, insurance, retail, and many others are more likely to deal with persistent transformation, as their strength has become their weakness, and disruptors are constantly finding new sources of value (Figure 2). During the pandemic, retail for example, was deeply impacted, with people unable to go shopping in person. Those retailers that had not adopted the right technologies or started their digital transformations were caught unprepared to deal with the massive changes.

Disruptability Index Industry Sector Matrix — 2018 results
0-1 scale (1 = most susceptible/disrupted)

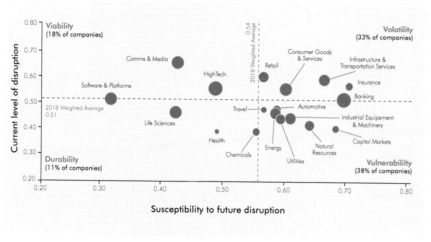

Figure 2. Disruptability Index Industry Sector Matrix — 2018 results. Source: Accenture Research.[19]

The pandemic has exacerbated the issues in most businesses, and those which were prepared leveraged the crisis to create opportunities to innovate quickly. Take Starbucks, for example. The organization was already in an ongoing digital transformation when the pandemic hit. It quickly changed priorities to implement new solutions to keep the business afloat. The Starbucks mobile app, used by customers to customize and pay for their orders, was considered a critical solution for when people were afraid to interact with each other, touch screens or stay inside the stores. Because it was prepared, Starbucks was able to navigate the uncertainty when the business scenario radically changed.[20]

In other sectors, those who were prepared had some characteristics in common. They were able to leverage emerging technologies such as data analytics and take advantage of 'technology as a service' to have quick access to what they needed.

Dematerialization and the 'as-a-service' business model is a reality, not just a trend anymore, since you have pretty much your life surrounded by "as a service" models (movies, books, news, mobility, clothes, etc.) that are challenging the principle of possession of goods in detriment of having the on-demand service.

The core principle here is pay per use, not possession. A good example here is cloud computing. Instead of investing thousands of dollars in data centers, networks, infrastructure, buildings, maintenance, etc., you have access to several services provided by large organizations such as Amazon AWS, Microsoft, Google, Oracle, just to name a few. Cloud computing enables storage, development tools, processing power, and several other applications that the organization can activate when needed and deactivate when not required. Done right, the cloud transformation will help the organization become more effective, innovative, and competitive.

Organizations do not have to heavily invest in equipment, staff, training, maintenance, and deal with outdated and depreciated technology. Research[21] shows that 80 percent of business executives look to cloud computing services as a means of mitigating business uncertainty and risks. There are many benefits of cloud technology as a service. It can help organizations accelerate and scale innovations, adapt at speed to changes, streamline operations, reduce costs, and drive business agility.

As a comparison, Figure 3 shows the rate of technology adoption before and after the pandemic. What is most interesting is the trend of adopting technology 'as a service,' leveraging the scalability and flexibility of cloud computing.

Overall rate of adoption

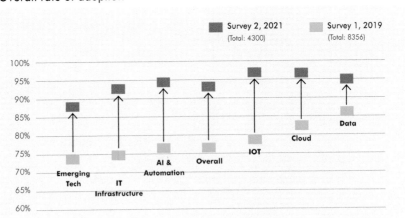

Figure 3. Overall rate of technology adoption before and after the Pandemic. Source: Accenture Research.[22]
Legend: Emerging tech: blockchain, extended reality, open source, 3D printing, robotics. IT Infrastructure: DevSecOps, serverless computing, cloud native applications, containers, docker and Kubernetes, microservice architectures, distributed logs/event hubs, react/event driven architectures, FaaS. AI & Automation: deep learning, machine learning. IoT: internet of things, edge/fog computing. Cloud: SaaS (software as a service), IaaS (infrastructure as a service), PaaS (platform as a service), hybrid cloud. Data: data lakes, repository, streaming/ real-time data, big data analytics.

To give an example, a large Italian multinational electricity and gas manufacturer and distributor implemented one of the largest virtualization projects on its telecommunications network to accelerate its digital transformation. This shift to the cloud contributed to reducing operating costs, by increasing the agility of the company's infrastructure. Now, its network connects over 1,000 sites on three continents and more than ten countries. It also contributed to a reduction in go-to-market time, costs optimization and improved operations. The company was able to quickly move over 37,000 employees to work remotely, providing secure access to applications and environment to continue its operations.[23]

There will be an exponential growth of offerings as a service after the pandemic especially in those business environments that need flexibility, scalability, and quality. Key recommendations to leverage technology as a service to support a hybrid environment and contribute to business agility are:

- Start right — begin with a clear strategy to use technology as a service to support the hybrid environment characteristics and business agility capabilities that you need. Like agility, technology is just the means to an end. Having a clear strategy to adopt technology will help an organization keep its focus on what matters, avoid unplanned costs and get more for its dollar.
- Leverage partnerships — choose wisely: you don't need to partner with just one provider, but you need to be mindful about the pros and cons of having multiple partners and services. Hybrid and multicloud environments are a reality but they also offer trade-offs that need to be managed. Be strategic about your core competences, do not try to internalize everything.
- Accelerate toward the new — technology leaders, also known as the 'high adopters' — the organizations that are massively adopting cloud and modern technologies — are now growing at 5x the rate of laggards (or low adopters). In 2019, this difference was 2x the speed of laggards.[24]
- Unlock growth and innovation — do not adopt these services just to cut costs. Adopt these services to boost growth and innovation through improving speed to market, better customer experience, testing new ideas and products quickly and cheaply, and identifying new revenue streams and business models.

- Mind the talent gap — the adoption of new technologies, as well as new processes and ways of working, will likely trigger the need to reskill and upskill your workforce. When the pandemic sped up, many organizations rushed to secure the best talent. In addition, mobility and flexibility came into perspective, since people now have access to opportunities everywhere.

Thriving in a persistent transformation environment will require a different set of capabilities and skills from senior executives. Building a hybrid environment, making agility pervasive and taking advantage of technology as a service will contribute to make organizations 'future ready.' Transformation is becoming more frequent and complex than ever. No matter how much organizations are prepared, they will need to stay alert to anticipate, adapt and accelerate changes to take advantage of opportunities and become more resilient.

About the authors

Edivandro Carlos Conforto is a managing director and Latin America lead of the Business Agility and Transformation Practice at Accenture. The author of a number of books and over 50 articles, published in business magazines globally, he is a world-renowned specialist with over 15 years of experience working with executives in different industry sectors in Brazil, EUA and Europe. Between 2013 and 2015, he lived in Boston, USA, where he attended a post-doctoral program at MIT focused on business agility. He holds a PhD and a master's degree in agile management and innovation from University of São Paulo. He is the first Brazilian to receive international recognition as a result of his contributions to agile management and business agility.

Juliana Mendes is a business agility and IT advisor, and principal director at Accenture. She has over 20 years of experience helping customers from multiple industries drive performance improvements and unlock their full potential using digital and advanced techniques to manage their organization and business decisions. A specialist in designing transformational solutions for complex problems, she studied IT project management at postgraduate level, with executive training in digital transformation and innovation at Harvard Business School and data driven consulting at Northwestern University, along with overseas specialization courses in organizational agility.

Footnotes

12 More information about being ready to remote work available at https://www.accenture.com/
cr-en/case-studies/about/ready-remote.

13 Accenture Research. Source: https://www.accenture.com/us-en/blogs/voices-public-service/
curious-about-returning-to-work-youre-not-alone

14 Arena, M.J. (2021), 'Adaptive Space: Shifting from structure to social design', *Management
and Business Review*

15 Bianchi, M.J., Conforto, E.C., and Amaral, D.C. (2021), "Beyond the agile methods: a
diagnostic tool to support the development of hybrid models", *International Journal of
Managing Projects in Business*, Vol. 14 No. 5, pp. 1219-1244.

16 Conforto, E.C., et al. (2014). *The building blocks of agility as a team's competence in
project management*. Massachusetts Institute of Technology. MIT research report available at:
https://scholar.google.ca/citations?view_op=view_citation&hl=en&user=AjLBjGkAAAAJ&cita
tion_for_view=AjLBjGkAAAAJ:hqOjcs7Dif8C

17 Conforto, E.C., et al. (2016). The agility construct on project management theory.
International Journal of Project Management, 34(4), 660-674. This article describes the
definition of agility and provide insights on how to measure it.

18 Fast track to future ready – Accenture Research, available at: https://www.accenture.com/
us-en/insights/operations/future-ready-operations

19 Accenture Research report. Breaking through disruption, June 26, 2019. Available at:
https://www.accenture.com/us-en/insights/consulting/business-disruption-innovation

20 This case is described in the research report "Accenture Technology Vision 2021", available
at: https://www.accenture.com/_acnmedia/PDF-145/Accenture-Tech-Vision-2021-Executive-
Summary-Geo-Version.pdf

21 Sky high hopes: navigating the barriers to maximizing cloud value. Accenture Research,
2020. https://www.accenture.com/_acnmedia/PDF-139/Accenture-Cloud-Outcomes-Exec-
Summary.pdf#zoom=40

22 Accenture Research. Make the leap, take the lead – tech strategies for innovation and growth.
Research report available at: https://www.accenture.com/_acnmedia/PDF-153/Accenture-
Make-The-Leap-Take-The-Lead-Report.pdf

23 ENEL beyond the cloud – more than a thousand sites connected by one of the world's largest
network virtualization projects. Accenture Newsroom: https://newsroom.accenture.com/news/
enel-beyond-the-cloud-more-than-a-thousand-sites-connected-by-one-of-the-worlds-largest-
network-virtualisation-projects.htm

24 Make the leap, take the lead – Tech strategies for innovation and growth. Accenture
Research, available at: https://www.accenture.com/_acnmedia/PDF-153/Accenture-Make-
The-Leap-Take-The-Lead-Report.pdf

How to survive in a world of perpetual transformations

CLAUDIO GARCIA

5

It took twenty years for the recorded music industry to fully recover its total sales from its peak in 1999, at least in absolute numbers (if adjusted for inflation, it would still take a few more years). All changed when file sharing peer-to-peer services became available on the internet, specifically Napster, which developed an interface in which it was easy to catalog and search for song files. In less than three years, it reached about 80 million users — that's half of Spotify's current number of paid users — sharing an unimaginable amount of song files for free. This was a significant revolution for an industry that, in the 40 years before Napster, had the cassette tape and the Compact Disc player — physical formats to store a tiny amount of music (usually 10-20 songs) — as its major technological advancements.

But Napster could not leverage its success. It was slaughtered by lawsuits from major record labels and artists angry with copyright infringements. After many losses in court, a little more than two years after its foundation, Napster shut down its peer-to-peer services. Since then, the company has tried other formats to stay alive and changed ownership many times — today it is owned by MelodyVR, a live music streaming platform — but never recovered the clout and popularity of its early years.

Napster is an essential part of the history of early internet entrepreneurship and a commonly used history of disruption. While it is far from a successful business story, Napster sowed the seeds of new behavior in the consumption of music. Even after the shutdown of the peer-to-peer service, users continued to shift from buying physical formats to downloading music based on their demand, supported by other alternative platforms and ever-improving internet bandwidth. In the recorded music industry, the bottom of revenues came in 2014. In some countries, that represented less than half of the peak of 1999 (not adjusted for inflation). So, Napster is a story of disruption. It put a whole industry through a process of reinvention which has lasted many years without yet reaching a happy ending. Even the most prominent global player in the field today, the streaming service Spotify, is still to show a profit.

As with many other stories of disruption, Napster shows that it is not easy to see where transformations are precisely coming from, which format they will take, and how long it will take an industry to find a new sustainable path. And yet, it is crucial to be ready for the unexpectedness of a world undergoing perpetual transformation, even if it is a rough path.

A transformation does not mean something better will automatically emerge.

The change of the consumer of music habits triggered by Napster was a misfortune for the recorded music value chain. It significantly reduced the size of the pie for everyone. Even though it is much easier to publish a new album nowadays, it is challenging even for a mid-sized artist (which means having songs streamed a couple million times) to make a decent living.

Similar dynamics can be seen in many other disrupted industries. The ride car revolution (Uber, Lyft, Didi, among others) brought significant transformation in the personal transportation industry. However, there's no clear winner since these players are still burning cash significantly to keep their operations working, and most traditional taxi businesses lost substantial market share. Or, another example, the food delivery industry, where around the globe, companies like Door-dash, Deliveroo, and Grub-Hub, despite massive adoption by users, are far from profitability. Even the surge in food delivery caused by the Covid pandemic was not enough to turn the financial statements of these companies green. In both these industries, there are still many questions about how sustainable the companies' relationships with drivers and delivery workers are — a critical element for the survival of their business models. Many reports question the working conditions and pay levels of workers in those industries. In some cases, this has led to legal complications which threaten already fragile business models.

This reality has been hidden by unrealistic valuations seen in stock markets and mainly in the venture capital industry. In times of extreme low cost of capital, liquidity has flown to riskier opportunities with apparently higher potential of return, many of them aggressive startups trying to disrupt traditional sectors. The tactics of those following the path of Uber, Lyft, and the food-delivery companies, are focused on aggressive client acquisition, most of the time driven by price subsidies to foster the rapid increase of adoption. These subsidies are difficult to remove to keep the same level of revenues and increase profitability.

In these industries, as in the music industry, the disruption has already affected the whole system that needs to adapt. Consumers who experience cheaper music, greater convenience, subsidized rides and so on, do not want to go back to the previous reality nor pay more. For organizations impacted by the changes of these pioneers, which in transformations are the large majority, there is no return to the golden times. Instead, they must rethink. They need their business to be more adaptable for this new — though not exactly fair — reality.

Innovations are built through a cemetery of failures; learn from them well to not become one.

Transformations happen because of many apparently disconnected events and less because of conscious intentions that organizations and their leaders believe will build their future.

In a recent conversation, a private equity executive shared how frustrated he was with the failure of many of their investments, some of them trying new business models. What made his disappointment worse was to see that many of the leaders behind these failures were somehow succeeding in other similar ventures. His realized that his private equity fund was effectively serving as a training platform to feed the success of others.

It is not a new discovery that failures can teach us much more than an eventual success. And that this happens many times without organizations being aware of or and actively acting to leverage it. Many of the innovations and brands we regard as successful are an outcome of many others that failed before them, and left remains absorbed by those who eventually succeeded. Highly innovative environments are those where more attempts, and consequently, failures happen. The sacrifice of many makes the whole system more robust. Platforms like Spotify and Apple Music are what they are because many others failed before them to find a new way to provide music experiences to users. They left successful features, experienced people, frustrated users, and many other valuable things for today's players.

Much has been said about the acceptance of failure in organizations. This is often misinterpreted as forgiving, forgetting, and moving to the next thing, when it should be seen as a rich and desired path to boost learning and wisdom. An even more significant opportunity, intentionally leveraged by very few is to learn from the failures of others outside their organizations, being appreciative of and honoring them rather than stereotyping them as losers, as many constantly do to protect their self-esteem and justify their choices.

Pay attention to where your clients are going — that is the real threat.

For artists, the advent of Napster threatened a big chunk of their incomes from sales of albums in physical formats. It also meant that new routes to fame were increasingly available and important. The British band Radiohead had never reached the top 20 in the U.S. Billboard ranking. But, in 2000, some of the songs from the new Radiohead album were leaked to Napster months before the album launch and were shared by millions of users. When launched, the album reached number one on the Billboard list. This was later attributed to the leak.

Many other bands noticed the opportunity to save them years of mailing physical demo tapes to fans, record labels, and concert organizers trying to find space to show their talents. Arctic Monkeys, now a well-known alternative rock band, learned their way through file-sharing, which ultimately helped them sign a contract for their first album. While many big-name artists like Metallica, Dr. Dre, and Madonna were focused on suing (rightfully) Napster for copyright violations, others were learning and benefitting from a transformation that had just started and would not stop. Many famous artists such as Shawn Mendes, The Weeknd, Adele, and Justin Bieber, would not be who they are today without benefitting from these accessible paths to reaching an audience. The new way became the standard.

None of this is instant. Compact Discs, even declining, were still selling significantly five years after the decline of Napster. Early detection and acceptance that these changes in habits could become the 'new normal' would allow companies and artists to try new possibilities. In parallel, efficient management of a declining business could generate enough cash for the transition.

The only way to notice these subtle movements is to stay close to those who your company exists for: clients. In times of perpetual transformation, that is the most effective way to observe trends and start learning how to adapt or even innovate with new possibilities. Many ventures are being launched every day with exciting solutions and new approaches to disruptive markets. But they are, in fact, a big distraction. What matters is where your clients are deciding to go. It can be to one of these new ventures. It can be to something completely different.

The best alternative to deal with complexity is through an effective diverse team.

Napster was a straightforward solution: each member had an available folder in their computers so millions of others worldwide could download files from it. But it mattered that the focus given by the founders was to easily catalog MP3 files (a popular digital format). Its founders were young computer hackers who had no previous experience with the music business. It didn't matter — the impact of this 'ingenuous' solution to the recorded music industry was massive. For artists and record labels, the means to make money and increase audiences were completely transformed. Besides good composition and finding spots for presentations, they now need to develop expertise in social media, video-streaming platforms, and search engines, to be minimally visible. They need to understand the intricacies of the constantly changing algorithms of these platforms, adjusting their communications, language, and even their compositions, so they can become attractive. For example, many reports suggest that as most algorithms tend to make recommendations based on similarities in the preferences of users, it has been more difficult for original pieces to thrive.

With new interventions, solutions, and ways to overcome the new challenges, it is a much more complex environment with significantly more different elements to interact with. To be effective, a company is required to dive into this complexity, and it can only do so through a diverse group of people. People are the ultimate source of capabilities. And organizations have the advantage of composing their teams to match the complexity of their environment. By not doing so, they are depending on luck. In the music industry, players are adjusting their operations to accommodate beyond their business and artistic casts, hiring technologists, statisticians, social media experts, and streaming specialists, all intended to increase their effectiveness in a new field.

But beyond the technical capabilities required to face complexity, companies need to absorb different perspectives about this reality, which is more subjective and difficult to tackle. It means that they need to accommodate profiles of people that have been in the social and technological context where the transformation is happening, people who breathe the changing reality of current and prospective clients.

The growing focus on diversity has (rightfully) focused on having a more equal and fair representation of society in an organization's workforce. This still requires the ability to leverage all these differences to benefit the business. Bringing together a more diverse group of people comes with the onus of more complexity to be managed. But it also brings much higher potential of matching the complexity of the environment through different points of view and capabilities that, if well managed, can trigger efficacy, creativity and increase the company's desired adaptability.

Mainstream management processes do not deliver this. Competence frameworks, selection, performance, evaluation, and promotion processes incentivize similar behavior and attitudes based on stereotypes of what is a 'talent' and definitions of organizational cultures that narrow the rich diversity that people could bring to their jobs.

Companies need to redefine their management systems to avoid the trap of having only people that fit their definitions of talent and organizational culture. Management systems and leadership environments must be capable of adding and promoting diverse capabilities. In a world of perpetual transformation, to match the complexity of transformations, adaptative advantages come from adding capabilities, not narrowing them.

Everybody wants to transform the world, but it is highly probable you will be changed by it.

For each disruption that transforms the world, ten of thousands of organizations will need to adapt to it. Yet, many are more interested in the former, ignoring that acknowledging the latter can mitigate the risks imposed on their organizations. Aside from a few exceptions, successful transformations mean, most of the time, adapting to survive and, maybe, thriving again.

Organizational leaders can give too much attention to things that will not make them more adaptable to an environment in perpetual transformation. The transformation of the recorded music industry is an example of how raw the path can be. And also an alert to areas that leaders need to pay more attention to:

- The genuine nature of transformations can be tricky and many times shows no clear light at the end of the tunnel. That requires organizations to honestly acknowledge it and be open to possibilities.
- The flow of the future follows the habits of clients who, on many occasions, do not want to go back to their previous experience. Follow them and try playing in the new paths they are moving along.
- To succeed, many have failed, honored, learned and absorbed their lessons. To do so is much cheaper and easier than many acquisitions and investments in 'innovative' bets companies do most of the time.
- The power of a diverse team needs to be intentionally leveraged — so stop narrowing it. Do an audit of your management processes, especially in people management. They might promise to deliver on the organizational strategy, but at the end are reducing its adaptability to the world.

The never-ending quest for adaptability should already be part of the organization's mindset and its design. Leaders can have high aspirations of transforming the world, but the reality is that it is much more common to be surprised by a world that is unpredictably moving ahead of most of us.

About the author
Claudio Garcia is based in New York where he is an entrepreneur and teaches at the School of Professional Studies, New York University.

Transforming for a sustainable future

MATT GITSHAM

Pressure is building within your industry about the negative environmental impact of a traditional manufacturing process. The implications for your organization are huge (and likely to be extremely costly). As a leader in the business, do you engage positively with the sector debate and take a leading role in attempts to find a solution or do you keep your head down and hope it will go away?

Employees in your organization are becoming increasingly vocal in their concerns about the possibility of modern slavery in the supply chain. As a leader, do you welcome their challenge and open up safe spaces for conversation and the co-creation of solutions — or do you attempt to stifle the debate?

As organizations start the process of building back better after the pandemic, these leadership dilemmas will arise more and more frequently. As we gradually come to terms with the 'new normal' and the challenges of living with COVID-19, the focus is starting to shift from emergency responses to a volatile situation to assessing what we may need to do differently in the longer-term.

Key to this transformation, will be taking urgent and ongoing action toward achieving net zero and tackling the wider sustainability and human rights agenda.

Multiple global crises were already upon us before the pandemic hit. At the same time as the virus was taking hold, the impact of the climate crisis was becoming ever more visible. 2020 began with images of Australia on fire. Summer 2021 brought record heat to the Western United States and Canada, wildfires to Siberia and extreme floods to Europe and China.

There have been other global ecological and human rights challenges too. Biodiversity and species loss have reached such a scale that scientists are warning the Earth is on the brink of a Sixth Mass Extinction, with more and more species being categorized as critically endangered or under threat. We are faced with pressing human rights challenges too, such as systematic discrimination against certain groups (witness the Black Lives Matter and #MeToo movements) and the 40 million people trapped in modern slavery today, many of these within corporate supply chains.

These are all crises that many people — NGOs, government leaders, business leaders — were already working together long before the Covid pandemic hit. Frameworks, like the UN Sustainable Development Goals and the Paris Climate Agreement, had been developed as roadmaps for the work that needed to be done.

One thing COVID-19 has taught us, however, is about the need to be better prepared and to build resilience to deal with the predictable, and other unpredictable shocks, that may emerge down the line. It has been a wake-up call about the need to build a recovery that doesn't just take us back to the status quo, but which sees us constantly transforming as we look to find ways of taking a more responsible and sustainable approach to the way we do business.

A commercial imperative

There's not just a moral imperative for organizations to take action, but a commercial one too. Corporates have for some time been facing increasingly loud calls, from customers, regulators, investors and employees, for a radical change in the way they operate. Customers are increasingly looking to deal with companies who can demonstrate green credentials and a concern for human rights across their supply chains. Employees increasingly want to work for organizations with a strong societal and sustainability track record, whose values and purpose echo their own. Reputations are at risk as pressure groups become increasingly vocal in their demands that organizations act on everything from reducing carbon emissions through to inclusion and gender and racial equality.

The UN Sustainable Development goals have been described as the world's biggest business opportunity, with economic opportunities of US$12 trillion a year[25] — equivalent to 10 percent of global GDP — available in four key economic areas alone.

Businesses are sitting up and taking notice, and recognizing they need to redefine corporate success beyond just delivering return on investment to shareholders, and toward delivering societal impact, resilience and a greater sense of shared responsibility for humanity's future.

A new organizational blueprint

What does this mean in practice for organizations who genuinely want to make the shift towards conducting sustainable, responsible business? First and foremost, it means going beyond lip service and compliance. It means abiding by international human rights norms and global environmental agreements, regardless of whether governments are enforcing them effectively. It means seeking opportunities for growth through innovation and bringing to market products and services that make a difference to global challenges. And it means taking a stance and speaking out if required — sometimes pushing governments for more regulation, for example, rather than fighting against it.

Some of the world's most influential companies are leading the way. Apple Inc, for example — one of the world's most valuable companies — announced at the height of the pandemic in July 2020 a plan to be entirely carbon neutral by 2030, including emissions from across its supply chain and product life cycle, with consequent implications for all companies seeking to be suppliers.

New approaches like these demand a new organizational blueprint, encompassing strategy, culture and mindset. So where does an organization start? How does the business decide which global challenges are the important ones to focus on? And how do leaders go about building the culture of responsibility that's needed to support the transformation?

The winning combination

The answer lies in a combination of strategy and leadership. The first step toward establishing a new strategic direction is to conduct a sustainability assessment, which will provide a map and compass to guide future action. This will help the organization assess exactly where it stands in relation to the sustainability agenda — and what it needs to do next.

The United Nations Sustainable Development Goals (17 of them) — which cover issues such as good health and well-being, gender equality, responsible consumption and production and climate change — are a good starting point.

Using these as a basis, organizations can draw up a 'long list' of challenges that are relevant to their business. They can then begin to hone this down by identifying those which have a current high impact (or a potential high impact) on the business, and mapping these against those challenges which are also of high interest and concern to stakeholders. With a clear picture in place and priorities identified, the focus can then shift to creating a culture which will enable action — which is where leaders come in.

Identifying the issues that matter and prioritizing

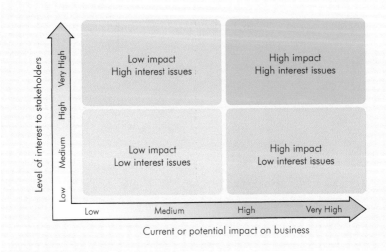

Source. Corporate Citizenship. Sustainability Strategy Simplified.

A changing role for leaders

As more and more organizations have engaged with helping address global sustainability and human rights challenges, so business leaders have found themselves adopting new leadership roles. As we seek to build back better, this leadership shift needs to accelerate.

At Hult Ashridge Executive Education, we've been leading a program of research on this changing role, talking with some of the CEOs at the forefront of the trend. Their experiences suggest that today's business leaders need a different mindset and a different skill set to their predecessors.

A generation ago, a leader's role was to keep their head down and focus on the numbers. Challenges in society were the job of political and activist leaders. For business leaders to get involved would be a distraction, would lack legitimacy and would end up adding cost to the bottom line.

But in today's world, business leaders need a different mindset to be successful. They need to see addressing societal and sustainability challenges as at the heart of their job description and not as a source of cost, but at the core of the way they add value. They are leaders in society as much as leaders of the business.

Rather than seeing a trade-off between doing good and making money, leaders need to aim to achieve each through the other.

Leading change inside and outside the organization

Our interviews (with CEOs and senior executives from more than 30 companies) showed that leaders are indeed beginning to think differently about the scope of their role. They recognize that they are responsible not just for leading cultural change within their organization, but also for leading change across their industry sector and wider society, often working in partnership with campaigners and other business and political leaders.

The chief executives we spoke to talked of seeing their own role in influencing change in their organizations in terms of opening up the space for others to behave differently — through the goals they articulated and the rationales they developed for pursuing them, the stories and people they celebrated, the conversations they started, the questions they asked, what they were seen to spend their own time doing, and which individuals and groups got recognized and rewarded and for what.

This new horizon to their role has required leaders to develop skill in areas that historically have not been a conventional part of their repertoire; contributing to public debate with an informed point of view, relating well with multiple constituencies, engaging in dialogue to understand and empathize with groups and communities with perspectives different to their own, and engaging in multi-stakeholder collaboration with unconventional partners.

Take consumer goods giant Unilever for example.[26] Former CEO Paul Polman launched Unilever's Sustainable Living Plan in 2010 , a 10-year strategy to double the size of the business by 2020 by setting targets such as helping a billion people improve their hygiene habits, bringing safe drinking water to 500 million people, doubling the proportion of the food portfolio meeting stringent nutrition standards, halving the greenhouse gas impact of Unilever products across their lifecycle and sourcing 100 per cent of raw materials sustainably.

Over the ten years of the implementation of this strategy, many of these targets were met and good progress was made on many others, and Unilever has become a benchmark for others to emulate. A corporate strategy with goals like this has required leading change within the organization, but also leading change in consumer behavior, leading change among suppliers and competitors across industry sectors and engaging with governments to lead change in policy frameworks.

Implications for talent management and development

Getting this new leadership role right is increasingly important for organizations. But to date, the extent to which they have ended up with people in leadership roles who can do this well has tended to be the result of chance rather than design.

We asked business leaders for their perspective on how it was that they and some of their peers had grasped the need to lead in this kind of way, while many of their other contemporaries were still operating from an out-of-date leadership blueprint.

While each individual's story was unique, the clear theme was that certain key experiences had been crucial in influencing and shifting perspectives. For some, it was formative experiences around upbringing, university and business school study. For others it was influential mentors or first-hand experiences like engaging with people living in poverty, personal experience of challenges like the impacts of climate change, or personal first-hand experiences of the changing interests of key stakeholders. Peer learning networks, like the UN Global Compact and World Business Council for Sustainable Development, for example, were also influential.

These stories have important implications for how organizations think about talent management and executive development. They suggest that more is required than just briefings and lectures on global trends and their commercial implications. Relationships and first-hand experiences are at the heart of what it takes for business leaders to build the emotional connection and commitment to put this agenda front and center of their work.

To foster the right kind of leadership capability in their organizations, HR, learning and development and organization development teams need to value these kinds of life experiences when making decisions about recruitment, career development and succession planning, and make sure they are embedded in the HR processes that underpin them. Not because they are 'nice-to-haves' that demonstrate a rounded individual, but because of the crucial contribution they make to developing a worldview, relational ability and the organizational culture now essential for organizations to survive and thrive.

There is clearly much work still to do. A study by the UN Global Compact and Russell Reynolds Associates[27] — the executive search firm — found that while 92 percent of business leaders believe integration of sustainability issues is critical to business success, only four percent of C-suite role specifications demand sustainability experience or mindsets.

Executive education for a sustainable future

If these personal, first-hand experiences are key to developing sustainable leaders, organizations need to think about how they can support this through their executive education programs.

Ashridge's research with organizations like IBM, HSBC, Lendlease, Interface, IMC Group and others suggests that more and more organizations are structuring their leadership development activities to include powerful experiential learning.

Initiatives have included giving senior executives the chance to develop relationships with people experiencing some of the world's most pressing challenges, as well as with the people working to address these challenges.

Organizations are also finding ways to help their leaders engage with new ideas which will help them make sense of the demands of the new business context, such as ecology, complexity, systems thinking and social constructionism.

Take Dutch multinational Philips for example. As part of its leadership development program, participants worked on projects to develop new commercial propositions which would also help to improve people's lives (in line with the organization's goal to improve the lives of three billion people a year by 2025).

One learning project, for example, challenged participants to develop proposals for serving rural communities in India with good business case potential and the ability to scale up. After spending time engaging first-hand with women in rural Indian communities as well as with health professionals and NGOs, the team developed an idea to use mobile communications technology to support remote diagnosis.

The result has become a thriving public-private partnership involving Philips, government and NGO partners. Health professionals now travel among rural communities with portable ultrasound, X-Ray and ECG testing equipment and send test results electronically to specialists in distant hospitals using mobile technology, who then liaise with the health professionals to discuss diagnosis via video-conference.

Singapore-based shipping conglomerate IMC Group is another example. Working with partners from the Global Institute for Tomorrow, the IMC Integrated Leadership Program for high potentials in the organization involves a week of classroom-based learning exploring socio-political and environmental trends, sustainable development and business, followed by a week of experiential immersion learning, tasking participants to develop a strategy that embraces the principles of sustainable development for a specific part of the business. One iteration of the program saw participants spend a week on one of the company's palm oil plantations in Kalimantan, Indonesia, engaging with local management, local workers, families in local communities and ecologists.

Facilitating learning

With pandemic concerns likely to disrupt travel and face-to-face personal contact for some time to come, opportunities for first-hand experiences will be harder to achieve, but there are numerous other ways to facilitate learning around global challenges. These might include virtual simulations, business challenge projects, and coaching and mentoring from leaders who have been at the vanguard of this change. There is also an opportunity to provide learning experiences that allow participants to connect virtually with stakeholder groups such as industry peers across the value chain, policymakers in governments and international institutions and activists in NGOs, trade unions and other civil society bodies.

Organizations need to support their leaders as they step into this new territory and begin to lead the necessary transformation, not least in developing psychologically safe environments so that those who are leading change are free to challenge corporate thinking and experiment with new approaches, without fear of negative consequences.

It is time for organizations to take this unique opportunity — indeed duty — to step up and play their part in developing a sustainable, responsible future for us all.

About the author

Matt Gitsham is Director of the Ashridge Centre for Business and Sustainability at Hult Ashridge Executive Education, part of Hult International Business School. Matt has led numerous research projects on business and sustainable development and human rights over nearly two decades at Hult Ashridge. Recent projects include exploring CEO perspectives on the implications of sustainability for business leadership; CEO lobbying for more ambitious government policy on sustainable development; and the role of business in shaping the UN Sustainable Development Goals (SDGs). He has collaborated with and advised well-known networks and organizations including the UN Global Compact, Unilever, IBM, HSBC, De Beers, Cemex and Pearson among others.

Footnotes

25   https://www.wbcsd.org/Overview/News-Insights/General/News/Achieving-the-Sustainable-Development-Goals-can-unlock-trillions-in-new-market-value

26   https://www.theguardian.com/sustainable-business/blog/unilever-green-credentials-sustainability

27   https://unglobalcompact.org/library/5745

Making perpetual transformation the norm

SUSIE KENNEDY

7

As well as dealing with rapidly evolving political, economic, technological and environmental changes, organizations are experiencing unprecedented internal and external pressures from multiple stakeholders. Here we look at some of the forces creating the need for continuous evolution and what organizations can do to make perpetual transformation the norm.

Shareholders, customers and employees are challenging leadership power and forcing organizations to change. Executive boards can no longer concern themselves with just shareholder return as shareholder activism increases in environmental, social, and corporate governance issues (ESG). In June 2021, activists reached what is regarded as a watershed moment as a small investment firm called Engine No.1 had a significant victory, gaining three seats on the board of ExxonMobil in a bid to speed up the company's energy transition.[28] In the same month, investors used activism to drive gender equality by requesting Microsoft publish an annual transparency report following misconduct allegations against its founder Bill Gates. The growth of social movements such as Black Lives Matter and #MeToo is increasingly likely to be on the activist agenda as social unrest creates economic risk.

Customer expectations and needs are rapidly changing. According to KPMG's Future of Retail report January 2021, customers now have greater power in the retail relationship.[29] On shifting to online shopping, they have exponentially increased their choice, making it challenging to retain them. Customers want businesses to have a purpose; to stand for something in line with their values and expectations. They expect companies to use social media, artificial intelligence and other technologies to engage and connect with them, giving immediate personalized experiences. They expect this same level of superior experience from any business. Research by Salesforce found that 80 percent of customers now consider the experience a company provides as important as its products and services.

Employee activism is on the rise, especially among millennials. A U.S. study found that four in 10 employees have spoken up to support or criticize an employer's actions over workplace and societal issues. For example, on 1 November 2018, some 20,000 staff at Google offices worldwide started walkouts protesting about the company's treatment of women. They demanded changes in how the firm dealt with sexual misconduct allegations, following the New York Times report that Google paid a high-profile executive $90 million after becoming aware of a sexual misconduct allegation against him.[30] On 9 June 2021, more than 60 former staff at the UK's largest craft brewer, BrewDog, posted an open letter on Twitter to the company, accusing it of fostering a toxic culture of fear and misogyny prompting its Chief Executive to apologize.[31] Open letters and other forms of activism urging leadership to listen have been used by employees of many companies, including Wayfair, Amazon, Adidas, Facebook, and Microsoft, to name a few.

The context in which organizations exist is perpetually changing, so organizations must evolve and be permanently "switched on" to transformation. Leaders can focus on three key areas to help achieve this:

- Managing stakeholder relationships
- Reflecting on organizational strengths
- Creating a culture that allows perpetual transformation to thrive.

Managing stakeholder relationships

When boards increase engagement with shareholders, both parties can benefit. Higher levels of engagement increase trust and lead to a more open flow of information which boards can use to be proactive in making leadership decisions. Boards should be pragmatic and recognize activists can be a valuable source of knowledge. London Business School's Ioannis Ioannou suggests boards should be unafraid of ESG challenges as they may find activist support for their strategy.[32] Similarly, former Chair and CEO of Vanguard, Bill McNabb , says boards should stay open and listen closely to what activists say even if they don't like it.[33] Better still, board members should step out of their comfort zone and think like an activist.[34]

Managing customer expectations means continuously providing the best possible experience so they will return. Organizations require information about their customer expectations, needs and experiences, and they need powerful internal systems and processes to deliver the desired service. Success means taking advantage of the latest technologies and investing in digital transformation, not as a one-off initiative but as a continuous improvement process in how the business operates. Organizations cannot remain switched on to continuous transformation if they do not have the supporting technology and internal processes.

There are right ways and wrong ways of managing the relationship with employee activists. The best methods involve getting closer to employees and engaging them in continuous transformation efforts. However, Professor Megan Reitz of Hult International Business School says that the more senior people are, the more likely they will fall into the optimism bubble, underestimating how activists feel. Consequently, CEOs may dismiss activism for rebellion and ignore growing discontent.[35] For a more successful outcome, leaders should listen deeply to employees, using channels that allow honest feedback about the organizational mood concerning the "big issues." Equipped with this knowledge, boards can discuss how these issues will impact the values of employees, customers and shareholders, allowing them to consider the consequences of their leadership decisions.

Reflecting on organizational strengths

The notion of maintaining perpetual transformation can be daunting, but it is certainly possible considering the incredible achievements of organizations during the COVID-19 pandemic. For example, on 19 March 2020, Pfizer's CEO, Alberta Bourla, challenged everyone at Pfizer to "make the impossible possible" by developing a vaccine ideally within six months, certainly by the end of the year, which they did. He reflects their success was due to an extraordinary team effort, and a can-do, mission-driven culture that will drive future innovation to new heights. Bourla says next time someone says something is impossible, he expects peers to say, "Look at what the COVID-19 vaccine group accomplished. If they could do that, we can do this."[36]

Routinely reminding the organization of its strengths helps to maintain the motivation and curiosity necessary for continuous evolution. For example, our research into leadership lessons from the COVID-19 crisis showed UK local government senior managers had high levels of resilience and resourcefulness and led with compassion. Their operational teams were adaptable and flexible, and because managers believed it was better to ask for forgiveness than wait for permission, innovations happened quickly. As they moved beyond the crisis to business as usual, they found it helpful to remember what they had achieved to avoid slipping back to old ways.

Creating a culture for perpetual transformation

The role of a leader is to create the conditions that enable the organization to adapt continually in a rapidly changing environment. Creating the appropriate culture involves addressing mindsets and management practices, including:

- Cultivating curious mindsets
- Using a common approach to managing transformation
- Building transformation teams.

Curiosity drives us to explore and pursue new experiences. It enables us to build knowledge, develop intellect, and grow relationships and creative capability. Therefore, it is essential to the success of a continuously evolving organization, as it brings significant improvements in innovation, learning, decision making, performance, problem-solving, teamworking, communication and well-being.

According to Professor Todd Kashdan at George Mason University, people express curiosity in different ways across five dimensions.[37] Individuals can use our Curio-5 assessment tool to measure their preferences across these dimensions and learn how to increase curiosity bandwidth. Leaders can take practical steps to cultivate curious mindsets in the workplace, including:

- Directly encouraging curiosity by asking simple questions such as "What are you curious about today?"
- Role modeling by embracing new experiences, asking questions, challenging thinking, being open, relaxed and playful.
- Encouraging people to think deeper and differently about challenges and opportunities they face.
- Helping teams to use better brainstorming and questioning to increase curiosity.
- Encouraging lifelong learning, inside and outside of work and a self-managed approach.
- Creating psychological safety where everyone feels comfortable speaking up with ideas, questions, concerns or mistakes.

The reported failure rate of large-scale change programs has been around 70 percent over many years. Research by McKinsey indicates that organizations are more likely to be successful when they address mindsets and put in place dimensions that will enable sustainable execution.[38] This includes using a disciplined, common approach to leading and implementing transformation, as change programs with governance structures are at least six times more likely to succeed. A disciplined approach promotes a common language with a consistent methodology that speeds up decision making and delivery. It creates energy and boosts confidence, providing a road map for planning and execution so that valuable time is not wasted on duplication or working out ways to plan and implement.

Our 3-D Approach to Organizational Change is one such approach that integrates the discipline of project management (PMI) with the psychology of change in a structured process. Successful change is managed in three phases, and is achieved by following steps for leading the change while managing multiple change projects and ensuring continuous communication throughout. The approach includes tools and assessments for each stage of the change process to enable planning and regular progress reviews by the transformation teams. Importantly, it is a repeatable process used for continuous transformation throughout the organization.

Successful implementation requires the discipline of attention of senior leaders to ongoing transformation and the discipline of execution by high-performing teams. McKinsey transformation metrics found top-performing companies had over twenty percent of their people involved in wide-scale transformation. Commitment from the top and ownership from the bottom is key to success. High-ownership levels are created when setting up high-performing implementation teams by allowing time for team members to build relationships with each other. They can use a common methodology to get on with the planning process, starting with identifying their own team purpose and goals. Maersk Global HSSE Improvement successfully deployed a team of transformation coaches using KBA's 3D approach to build global high-performing teams, who in turn, were responsible for driving a "safety first" culture worldwide.

The above summarizes some of the forces pressurizing organizations to change and the tools leaders have at their disposal to create a culture for continuous transformation or ongoing evolution. Arguably, there is nothing inherently new in the overall approaches to change management, but there is a step-change in the need to focus on managing stakeholder relationships, creating the right mindsets and using a disciplined approach widely, in order to make perpetual transformation the norm.

However, critical to the success of any transformation is the behavior of leaders. A 2019 McKinsey report on transformation metrics suggests that leaders have significant influence over the success (or failure) of their company's transformations. Research shows 86 percent of leaders claim to role model behavioral changes, yet only 53 percent of the people who report to them agree.[39] So it is the leader's primary responsibility to routinely gain good feedback about their impact and ensure they espouse the behavior changes they seek of others. In the words of Peter Drucker, "You cannot manage other people unless you manage yourself first."

About the author

Susie Kennedy is senior partner of KBA Solutions Limited, which she founded in 1993. KBA specializes in change leadership consulting and executive development. She has contributed to the Thinkers50 books, *Transforming Beyond the Crisis* and *The Transformation Playbook*. Susie is Program Director for KBA's Institute of Leadership and Management Strategic Leadership program for senior managers, with programs in the University of Cambridge, Premier Foods and nationally for UK local government at King's College London.

Footnotes

28 Forsdick, S., (2021). "What's next for activist shareholders after ExxonMobil victory?" *Raconteur*. 18 June. [online] Available at: https://www.raconteur.net/corporate-social-responsibility/activist-shareholders-corporate-governance/ [Accessed 4 August 2021].

29 KPMG, (2021). *Future of Retail*. January. [online] Available at: https://assets.kpmg/content/dam/kpmg/xx/pdf/2021/01/future-of-retail.pdf [Accessed 4 August 2021]

30 Lee, D., (2018). "Google staff walk out over women's treatment." BBC. 1 November. [online] Available at: https://www.bbc.co.uk/news/technology-46054202 [Accessed 4 August 2021]

31 Evans, J., (2021). "Former BrewDog staff accuse company of 'culture of fear' and misogyny". *Financial Times*, 10 June.

32 Forsdick, S., (2021). "What's next for activist shareholders after ExxonMobil victory?" *Raconteur*. 18 June. [online] Available at: https://www.raconteur.net/corporate-social-responsibility/activist-shareholders-corporate-governance/ [Accessed 4 August 2021].

33 McNabb, B., Charan,R. & Carey, D., (2021) "Engaging with your Investors". *Harvard Business Review*. July-Aug 2021

34 Weinstein, G., de Wied, W. S. & Richter, P., (2019). "The Road Ahead for Shareholder Activism". Harvard Law School Forum on Corporate Governance. 13 February. [online] Available at: https://corpgov.law.harvard.edu/2019/02/13/the-road-ahead-for-shareholder-activism/[Accessed 4 August 2021]

35 Reitz, M., Higgins, J. & Day-Duro, E. (2021). "The Wrong Way to Respond to Employee Activism". *Harvard Business Review*. 26 February [online] Available at: https://hbr.org/2021/02/the-wrong-way-to-respond-to-employee-activism [Accessed 4 August 2021]

36 Bourla, A., (2021). "The CEO of Pfizer on Developing a Vaccine in Record Time". *Harvard Business Review*. May-June

37 Kashdan, T.B., Disabato, D.J., Goodman, F.R., & McKnight, P.E. (in preparation). "The five-dimensional curiosity scale revised (5DCR): Briefer subscales while separating general and covert social curiosity".

38 Keller, S & Schaninger, B., (2020). "How do we manage the change journey?" [online] Available at: https://www.mckinsey.com/business-functions/organization/our-insights/how-do-we-manage-the-change-journey [Accessed 4 August 2021]

39 Keller, S & Schaninger, B., (2020). "How do we manage the change journey?" [online] Available at: https://www.mckinsey.com/business-functions/organization/our-insights/how-do-we-manage-the-change-journey [Accessed 4 August 2021]

An essential framework for continuous innovation

KAIHAN KRIPPENDORFF

In the early 1800s, Hudson's Bay, a Canadian trading company, was facing collapse because a competing trading company, the North West Company, had adopted a new distribution strategy. By moving trading posts closer to customers, North West established a more flexible, decentralized management structure. Hudson's Bay's centralized bureaucracy hindered the company's reaction time, and by 1809 the company seemed destined to close. In that year, however, Hudson Bay's ownership changed hands. The new leadership quickly copied its rival's approach, moving trading posts nearer to customers and decentralizing operations.

By breaking through rigidity to react to a changing environment, the new owners saved the company.[40] In time, Hudson's Bay overcame its rival, merging with it ten years later, and survived as the Hudson's Bay Company, considered today to be the oldest surviving commercial enterprise in Canada. The ability to adapt and transform quickly proved essential to the organization's survival.

The lessons of Hudson's Bay's success are even more poignant today. In 2020, most of us experienced the greatest moment of change we are likely to experience in our lifetimes. When the COVID-19 pandemic hit, across industries and across markets, it was clear that adapting quickly and creatively to a changing environment is fundamental to a company's ability to survive and thrive. Almost overnight, brands pivoted to launch new offerings, institute remote working environments, and shift their services online.

Rather than slowing down in the post-pandemic world, change is picking up speed and becoming a constant. New technologies are being adopted faster, and disruption — by competitors, technological innovations, or unforeseen external forces — is ever-present. To survive in the future, your organization needs a strategy that can adapt and flex with the pace of change; one that offers creative options to keep you among the disruptors, rather than the disrupted, and that opens up space for continuous innovation and perpetual transformation.

The OODA Loop

John Boyd was one of the U.S. military's most brilliant strategists.[41] Today, he is known only to a small community of military tacticians and students of military methods. But his insights have come to define the basis of modern warfare.

During the Korean War, Boyd served as his squadron's commander and tactics instructor. Their F-86 jet fighters yielded less firepower or thrust than their opponents' MIGs, yet Boyd's pilots averaged a 10:1 kill ratio against their enemies. Throughout much of Boyd's career as an instructor, advisor, military theorist, and fighter pilot, he maintained a running bet that with forty seconds in the air he could beat any pilot in aerial combat. "Forty-second Boyd," as he came to be known, never lost this bet.

Asked to explain his methods, Boyd developed a theory of conflict that is now shaping militaries all over the globe. Central to his theory is that the entity — the squadron, army, company, government — that adapts fastest to changing events wins. He specifically identified four interdependent phases an organization or organism must pass through to adapt to changing reality: observation, orientation, decision, and action (the OODA loop, or Boyd cycle). To beat your competition, then, you must cycle through your OODA loop faster than them and/or hinder their ability to cycle through theirs. In Boyd's terminology, you must get "inside the enemy's OODA loop."

Boyd's principle has been at work for millennia, determining winners and losers on battlefields and in corporate conflicts. Master tacticians from Alexander the Great to Sun Tzu have demonstrated how the ability to adapt faster than the enemy can alter the outcome of a battle. And as the Hudson's Bay story illustrates, there is evidence of cycle time being a determinant of competitiveness in business as early as the turn of the nineteenth century. So, what does Boyd's theory teach us about perpetual transformation? Taking the four OODA elements in turn:

Observe

Due to the highly structured nature of organizations, most struggle to consistently respond creatively and quickly when their environment changes. Companies stifle creativity by relying too heavily on logical methods — they assume that since a strategy has worked in the past, it will work in the future. This results in repetitive, risk-averse strategies that fail to inspire innovation and transformation.

Through my work, which has spanned over two decades of strategy consulting workshops, training more than 5,000 clients in strategic-thinking agility, and researching several books, my colleagues and I have recognized common barriers to strategic innovation. One of the most prevalent hurdles that keeps companies from innovating is that they fail to observe that their environment has changed, and that new opportunities or threats have emerged. The reasons for this failure to observe are manifold, some of which I address below. What is important to understand is that most companies that have historically overcome disruption did so because they recognized and executed strategic options that their competitors would not, long before others even observed change might be on the way.

Hon Hai Precision Industries, for example, has become one of the world's largest electronics manufacturers, serving clients such as Dell, Apple, Cisco, Nokia, and Sony, and averaging 50 percent annual revenue growth over the last decade. Hon Hai achieved this by observing an industry dynamic emerge before others. In 1974, at a time when most electronics manufacturers were busy producing consumer electronics, Hon Hai was founded as a plastics manufacturer. Toward the end of the 1970s, however, it noticed an emerging trend. Because the company was located in Taiwan, the outskirts of this emerging trend, Hon Hai was one of the first to observe computer firms increasingly seeking to outsource production in Asia. As a result, in 1981, Hon Hai began producing computer connectors for a relatively unknown, six-year-old company called Microsoft. As Microsoft grew into one of the largest corporations in the world, Hon Hai enjoyed the pull of Microsoft's wake. By observing what few others were close enough to notice, Hon Hai took an early role in the emerging computer revolution. Today, Hon Hai produces $16 billion per year in revenues.[42]

Start at the edges

Like Hon Hai, your chances of outthinking your competition greatly improve if you can observe emerging trends before they do. Columbia Business School professor and globally recognized strategy and innovation expert, Rita McGrath has extensively researched how companies can predict and respond to environment changes, or *inflection points*, before they happen. She references former Intel CEO, Andy Grove, who observed, "When spring comes, snow melts first at the periphery, because that is where it is most exposed."[43]

McGrath argues that inflection points are not completely random — they can be observed and anticipated if we learn to look in the right places. To prevent being blindsided by rapid change, she recommends encountering the "edges." Rather than developing your strategy while locked away in a boardroom with a team of C-suite leaders, put yourself in contact with customers, employees, and other key stakeholders. Observe and uncover their pain points. Interact with diverse audiences and perspectives. Then, to ensure that your organization can act on these observations, empower and put trust in small agile teams that can move quickly and try new things. Remove bureaucratic corporate systems and red tape that weigh down decision-making and reporting processes.

Zoom out, then zoom in

John Hagel, the highly respected management consultant and founder of Deloitte's Center for the Edge, told me: "If you look back 20 or 30 years, strategy was about understanding your company's specific position in an industry to generate a fixed amount of value. Today, the world is much more dynamic." The boundaries between industries are becoming blurred — retailers are entering the banking industry,[44] big tech players are opening beauty salons,[45] and auto industry leaders are launching rockets into space.[46]

Hagel warns that a big shift is underway. "If you zoom out 10 to 20 years and you think you're going to be the same business that you are today, go back to the table."

He offers the concept, "zoom out/zoom in." Look ahead to your ten-to-twenty-year horizon and imagine, based on your observations and market insights, what your market or industry will look like. What are the big opportunities that you could target? Then zoom in to the next six to twelve months, what are the two or three initiatives that you could pursue that would have the greatest impact on moving you forward into the future?

Key questions to ask

To outthink your competition and market, it helps to put in place an information network that can feed you early warning signs of critical changes. Ask yourself the following questions:

- What competitive, market, technological, socio-demographic, or regulatory developments should I look for?
- What are the "leading indicators" I would expect to see change before these developments appear?
- Am I currently able to observe these leading indicators?
- If not, where does this information reside and how can I monitor it?

To prepare for a strategy brainstorming session, gather as much trend data on these leading indicators as would be useful. Much of this information may already reside inside your company. Indeed, we have found that corporations often gather more information than they can process and so are surprised to find that they are already collecting many of the leading indicator data they need. By triangulating data organized from seemingly unrelated areas of your operation, you may pinpoint what you need.

Orient

Often, companies that have successfully observed that their environment has changed fail to orient (or reorient) themselves to the implications of this change. We may observe clouds forming, for example, but fail to make the mental leap to consider the implications, that rain may soon fall. When I worked at McKinsey & Company, we were taught to continually ask, "so what?"

With your leading indicator data from the previous step in hand, it is critical that you think through the potential implications, especially if you are content with your current future because otherwise your change efforts will lack momentum.

Consider the case of the apparel company Puma, for example. In the decade beginning in 1995, Puma grew nearly twice as fast and was nearly twice as profitable as its peers. A troubled company in the early 1990s, Puma's recovery can be traced directly to the fact that board members had grown so discontented with the company's performance that they were prepared to make a radical strategic shift. They replaced the top management and embarked on a bold new strategy — one centered on fashion rather than athletic performance.

The company's rival Reebok faced similar financial troubles around the same time that Puma transformed its strategy, but because Reebok's performance was good enough to offer the company's leadership hope, it never swallowed what was required to transform. In 1994, Puma's revenues were just 8 percent of Reebok's. A little over ten years later, Puma had significantly closed this gap, reaching about 50 percent of Reebok's revenues.[47]

Identify patterns

Your capacity to orient (and reorient) is based on your ability to observe weak signals and put them together to identify patterns. In his book *The Pan-Industrial Revolution*,[48] Richard D'Aveni foreshadows the rise of a new sort of commercial entity. He argues that technologies like additive manufacturing or 3-D printing will expand beyond disrupting individual industries and will dismantle the concept of industries as we know them. Firms will be able to produce bicycle parts one minute, then automobile equipment the next. Later that same day, they might make parts for ships or drones. What should we call a company that can make all these things? Pan-industrial is D'Aveni's term, and he argues that firms need to be able to quickly flex and adapt the scope of their business.

Innovate around the core

While orienting yourself to observed changes may seem dizzying, computer scientist and organizational theorist, David Robertson offers reassurance that innovation is closer and easier to grasp than it appears. Rather than being a sudden stroke of creativity, innovation is often about observing the customer experience and rethinking how you work the products and solutions you already have into addressing seemingly incremental customer pain points. He argues that Steve Jobs was not a disruptor and that the iPod was not intentionally a product to revolutionize music; Jobs simply realized that life was becoming more digital and difficult to manage, so he helped people bring their music into the Mac system to be organized. To inspire continuous transformation, Robertson recommends observing what people are trying to do with your product and digging down to find out how you can help them to get more value out of it.

Key questions and exercise

1. Just as addicts will not seek rehabilitation until they reach "rock bottom," you and your team's creativity will remain bottled unless you reach a point of discontent. The easiest way to achieve the requisite discontent is to assess your future from an detached perspective. Ask yourself:
    - What would an outsider say our future looks like?
    - How would an outside analyst project our future revenues and profits?
    - Does the future to which you are headed inspire you?

If you find the imagined future uninspiring or, better yet, scary, rejoice, because you now have the chance to design a new one.

2. Next, imagine your desired outcome. Disregard past performance and the previous questions, and answer the following:
   - Where do I want my organization to be in the long term? What will our company and industry look like? (I have found five years to be appropriate in most situations.)
   - What three key metrics will indicate that we've achieve our long-term vision?
   - What is our near-term ideal? What must be true in the near-term for us to know we will realize our long-term ideal? (In most cases, the near-term is six to twelve months from now.)
   - What metrics will capture our near-term ideal?

3. Consider the gap between your current and near-term ideal. What strategic question, once answered, will lead you to achieving your near-term ideal? It should be specific, measurable, and have a definite time limit. For example, Tesla's strategic question asked, "How can we double the number of electric vehicles sold in the world and ensure that 80 percent of them use Tesla technology in three years?"

4. Once you have your ideal vision in place, dissect your challenge. Think carefully about what you need to do to get to your near-term ideal, and break the process into steps. You should feel that if you accomplish everything listed, you will achieve your goal. In the Tesla case, the company might break down the problem into three pieces: technology, cars, and drivers. The rationale for this breakdown is that as long as we can get our technology into enough electric cars and get drivers to buy them, we can double electric vehicles sold and achieve an 80 percent share.

5. Continue to break down your processes until you have identified a leverage point that you have not considered before. Select one key issue to focus on immediately.

6. The more options or solutions you and your team recognize, the more likely it is that you'll find one that works. Examine your challenge and write down all possible resolutions. In my workshops, participants often generate between 50 and 250 possible ideas. Don't discount ideas even if they seem foolish or impossible.

Decide

Now that you have created lots of ideas, your next challenge, the third part of the OODA cycle, is to decide which ones you will execute. Your goal is to reach strategic clarity and ensure that you have chosen the most disruptive strategy. Be careful not to ask, "Which ideas could I see working?" By triggering this visualization process, you are really asking, "Which ideas have I seen work in some other context?" This usually leads you back to the most obvious or familiar solution and will not result in the transformative innovation you desire.

Technology can be supportive in helping us avoid falling back on old ways of thinking. Artificial Intelligence expert, Ash Fontana proposes that AI can be used as a tool in decision-making.[49] In many cases, employing AI can help you decide more quickly or more confidently. Ask yourself, could AI and automated processes help me to make the decision I need to make better than I can make it right now?" By leveraging technology to your advantage, you can avoid most human error caused by fear or other emotions.

Key questions to ask

Given the future we desire, what options should we consider?
For each idea you generated, ask:
- What is the impact if we could successfully execute this idea?
- How easy will it be for us to execute?

Pick three to seven ideas that you are committed to either executing or validating.

Act

Now we come to the final crucial element of the OODA cycle. Your strategy is not what you say you will do; it is what you do. You have not created a strategy unless your intentions are translated into actions on the front line. In the end, what you do — how you treat your customers, from where you source your product, through which channels you distribute — must match what you intended.

The final step involves aligning roles, measurements, incentives, and communication. You must redefine roles to ensure people are able to take actions on the front line that are consistent with your new strategy. You then establish a set of measures to judge how well you are succeeding or failing.

Many of the strategy executives I work with note that the measurements used to judge transformation efforts should not be the same ones that judge the success of existing operations. Transformation by its nature requires risk and failure. Align incentives that reward these unique innovation measures. Finally, develop a compelling message and communication plan to ensure that all stakeholders are familiar with your new strategy.

Key questions to ask

- Which key stakeholders will be involved in deciding whether to act on your idea?
- How easy is it for you to influence them?
- What is their current disposition to your idea?
- What do you know about them?
- What message will encourage them to do what you want them to do?
- How can you engage them with your message?

Repeat

You have now transformed your strategy. But you are not finished, because the loop never ends. You observe the results your new strategy is producing, orient yourself to whether you are winning, brainstorm options and decide which to pursue, and act on your new strategy again. And again.

Hudson's Bay did not out-survive almost all other North American companies of its age through its deft adaptation in the early 1800s. It has cycled through OODA loops many times over the years. Companies that establish the capability to work through this process creatively and quickly do not only survive — they turn change into their competitive advantage.

About the author

Dr. Kaihan Krippendorff is the founder of the growth strategy consulting firm Outthinker. A former McKinsey & Co. consultant, he is the author of five business strategy books, most recently *Driving Innovation from Within*. He was named on the Thinkers50 Radar list of the most exciting up-and-coming thinkers.

Footnotes

40 https://www.canadiangeographic.ca/article/untold-story-hudsons-bay-company

41 Grant T. Hammond, *The Mind of War: John Boyd and American Security* (Smithsonian Books, 2001).

42 https://www.honhai.com/en-us/press-center/events/monthly-revenues/583

43 https://www.ritamcgrath.com/wp-content/uploads/2019/03/Snow-Melts-From-The-Edges.pdf

44 https://www.fastcompany.com/90658779/how-walgreens-and-walmarts-new-banking-ventures-will-shake-up-finance?partner=rss&utm_source=twitter.com&utm_medium=social&utm_campaign=rss+fastcompany&utm_content=rss

45 https://blog.aboutamazon.co.uk/shopping-and-entertainment/introducing-amazon-salon

46 https://www.cnbc.com/2021/08/03/elon-musk-photos-show-spacex-rolling-out-starship-rocket-booster.html

47 https://outthinker.com/wp-content/uploads/2021/03/a-manual-for-outthinking-the-competitionv3.pdf

48 Richard D'Aveni, *The Pan-Industrial Revolution* (Houghton, Mifflin, Harcourt, 2018).

49 https://outthinker.com/podcast/?wchannelid=jxermuwnpf&wmediaid=03zrg7emsx

Strategic explorations:
The wellspring of corporate renewal and longevity

JEFFREY KUHN

From the ancient writings of Herodotus to the mosquito-infested travails of Juan Ponce de León during the Age of Exploration, for centuries humans have sought to discover the Fountain of Youth–a curative spring that can turn back the hands of time and restore the vitality of those who bathe in its magical waters.

In the 1990s, at the twilight of the Industrial Era, a pack of sport-coat-clad explorers embarked on a similar quest: to discover the corporate fountain of youth, a concept that had caught the attention of senior business leaders facing the dual challenge of increasing competitive intensity and decreasing corporate life spans. Armed with catchy titles like *Built to Last* (1994) and *The Living Company* (1997), these modern-day adventurers sought to crack the code of corporate longevity at the dawn of the Digital Age.

The case examples in these books are, of course, dated, but the prescriptions offered in these tomes, such as establishing *big hairy audacious goals* (moonshots in Google parlance) and *try a lot of stuff and keep what works* (moving fast and breaking things in Facebook-speak) have influenced a generation of business thinkers and leaders grappling with the perennial question of how to lead a *living company* that is *built to last* in an era in which corporate life spans can be measured in dog years.

The taming of the new

The 1990s were a pivotal period in economic history and in the field of strategic management in general. The twin forces of globalization and digitization had gained critical mass, eroding barriers to entry and giving rise to new competitors with disruptive business models. Suddenly, leaders of established firms found themselves fighting tooth and nail in a competitive landscape characterized by deep complexity, high uncertainty, and transient advantage.

In the wake of declining corporate life spans (as reflected in average S&P 500 tenure, a proxy of market dynamism) coupled with the sanguine writings of Collins and Porras (*Built to Last*) and Arie de Geus (*The Living Company*), the concepts of organizational renewal and longevity began to take center stage.

A new breed of strategists also entered the fray during this period: the game changers, a rowdy band of thinkers who drew inspiration from Charles Darwin and Joseph Schumpeter and challenged the sacred creeds of strategy, especially those promulgated by Michael Porter — the patron saint of positioning. Influenced by Gary Hamel and C.K. Prahalad's frame-breaking concept of competing for the future and Richard D'Aveni's seminal writings on hypercompetiton, corporate strategy abandoned its canonical roots of creating barriers to competition and evolved into an imaginative, expeditionary-based pursuit of overturning industry conventions, playing with market boundaries (rather than playing within market boundaries), and cold-cocking unsuspecting competitors with a rapid-fire succession of strategic moves that neutralize points of differentiation, eroding long-held market positions.

The era of dynamic corporate strategy had arrived.

Industry metabolism: The strategic context of organizational renewal

Organizations, like all living organisms, must possess an innate ability to continuously renew their value-creating capacity to counter the deleterious forces of senescence–the gradual deterioration of cellular function (i.e., aging)–that occurs in all living organisms.

During periods of market upheaval, steady, evolutionary-based renewal through continuous improvement is insufficient. It progresses too slowly and is not designed for step-changes in the competitive environment. In periods of upheaval, organizational renewals must take the form of metamorphoses (a change from one form to another, such as a tadpole to a frog) through a deliberate process of apoptosis (the programed death of senescent cells) and biogenesis (the production of new, healthy cells).

The rate by which organizational renewal (or metamorphosis) needs to occur varies greatly by industry, market, and organizational context. Awareness of the broader landscape of organizational renewal is a key contextual consideration for strategic leaders. A renewal model that works beautifully at Netflix could trigger an acute allergic reaction at ExxonMobil.

To address these contextual considerations, when I teach executive education programs on strategic leadership, I often introduce the concept of *industry metabolism* to represent the rate at which a particular industry or competitive arena matures (moves up the s-curve) and morphs into a new form.

To illustrate, highly regulated, capital-intensive industries with formidable entry barriers tend to have slow metabolic rates that follow linear, evolutionary trajectories. As a result, they mature and morph into new forms s-l-o-w-l-y. Big oil, for example, has essentially operated with the same business model since its inception more than a century ago. Consequently, leaders in these industries think in terms of multidecade capital investments and yields, with disciplined operational management functioning as a stabilizing force to reduce variance and costs, optimize physical assets, and maximize shareholder returns. The future looks a great deal like the past in these industries so there is little perceived need in the executive wing to tinker with a proven success model. Continuous improvement will suffice. Assuming the market environment remains stable, these efforts can sustain a firm's market position for decades. However, things can quickly go awry if the metabolic rate suddenly increases and the firm is forced to switch its strategic posture from being better to being different.

In contrast, enterprises in digitally based industries, with low entry barriers, have significantly higher metabolic rates and tend to mature and morph into new forms rapidly, often with unpredictable, nonlinear evolutionary trajectories.

Netflix, for example, has reinvented its business three times (from shipping DVDs by mail, to video streaming, to creating original content) since its founding in 1997. Netflix recently announced a new gaming business; presumably to counter the recent influx of big-name players, such as Disney, Apple, and HBO Max, into the video streaming business, which will inevitably commoditize this competitive arena.

Pure play digital firms like Facebook and Netflix have a much different renewal landscape and challenge than industrial colossuses. In these market arenas, the future bears little resemblance to the past, and inertia and institutional memory are often a liability, especially if the game changes suddenly. In market arenas that mature and morph into new forms rapidly, imagination and creativity are the lifeblood of the enterprise—the élan vital of continuous renewal and regeneration.

Acceleration and turbulence can inflict considerable pain on firms that built their empires in the twentieth century and are suddenly forced to play a different, digital game. Kodak comes to mind. Beginning in the 1970s, it began a steady, multidecade decline amid aggressive market share competition from Fujifilm, instant photography developed by Polaroid, protracted antitrust litigation, and the sudden, exponential growth of digital photography in the late 1990s (which, ironically, it had invented in its own research labs decades earlier). The knockout blow, however, came on June 20, 2007, when Apple, Silicon Valley's equivalent of Mike Tyson and Kodak's former partner in digital photography, launched the iPhone, bringing a swift, painful end to the era of point-and-shoot digital cameras in the consumer market. Few firms could survive a drubbing like that.

Why good companies go bad

There are myriad reasons why successful companies are unable to adapt their enterprises to transformational market shifts and cascade into rapid decline:

- Structural and cultural inertia
- Fear of cannibalizing the core business
- Stick to your knitting syndrome
- The curse of success
- Missing or dismissing the weak signals of change
- Frozen mental models
- Short-termism and incrementalism
- Lack of foresight and imagination

However, these are all symptoms of the same underlying disease: an absence of strategic leadership.

In most cases of organizational decline, the market signals were clear. The firms were not blindsided by the future. The executives saw the clouds gathering on the horizon but underestimated the ferocity of the storm and the speed with which it would arrive. Eyes wide shut, they were too busy managing quarterly results and fighting over a quarter point of market share with an archrival and lacked the foresight and imagination to envision the customers, businesses, and industries of tomorrow. They were trapped in the denominator management box.

Trapped in the denominator management box

As illustrated in Figure 1, leading with a long-term perspective is an exercise in paradox, a high-wire act that balances top-line growth and bottom-line profitability while managing today and creating tomorrow. Few disagree with this framework, but over the years, I have observed that the comfort zone for many managers is the lower-left quadrant: managing today and maintaining bottom-line profitability. This is the Sisyphean world of denominator management that is essential to optimizing the core business and maximizing short-term results. But keep this in mind: an inordinate focus on the denominator can leave a firm vulnerable to exogenous threats (and missed opportunities), especially if this is the only arrow in their quiver.

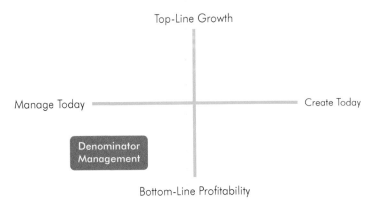

Top-Line Growth

Manage Today ———————————— Create Today

Denominator
Management

Bottom-Line Profitability

Figure 1

As an organization matures, its ethos often shifts from possibility and growth to scarcity and profit-protection, leading to short-termism and incrementalism. Left unchecked, these forces can engulf organizations, suppressing the imaginative thinking essential to long-term value creation and survival.

To illustrate, ask any group of managers to cut costs by 10 percent, and, without pause, they'll fire up their laptops and get to work delayering, reorganizing, outsourcing, offshoring, and nearshoring — classic denominator management. Now, ask the same group of managers to grow top-line revenues (the numerator) with new-to-the-company sources (the upper-right quadrant in Figure 1) and you'll likely get a blank stare. Why? They're not conditioned to think this way. Years of eking out slow, single-digit growth in mature markets has conditioned these managers to think in safe, incremental terms to protect short-term profits and keep investors happy. They have spent the bulk of their careers running full speed on the operational treadmill and solving complex organizational problems, rather than creating the growth platforms of tomorrow.

Problem-solving and creating are different activities requiring different cognitive capabilities and modes of thinking. Problem-solving involves fixing things and making them go away. Creating involves bringing something new into existence. Problem-solving draws on concrete, analytical modes of thinking (breaking things into parts for analysis), whereas creating draws on abstract, generative modes of thinking. Envisioning markets and businesses that don't yet exist requires immense foresight, as well as high conceptual and creative capacity — in other words, imagination. When thrust into strategic roles, operationally oriented managers often struggle with broad conceptual thinking. They can speak at length concerning KPIs and inventory turns — concrete modes of thinking — but they have difficulty finding their footing when asked to think and lead strategically with long-term, external perspectives, rather than from the internal purview of operations. Years of slogging on the operational treadmill have etched deep grooves into their cognitive architecture.

Increasing strategic and organizational complexity also drives short-termism and incrementalism. Paradoxically, digital technologies have increased productivity and improved our quality of life immensely, but they also have led to a dramatic rise in complexity — socioeconomic, technological, customer, channel, competitive, and organizational — that places immense cognitive demands on leaders, widening the gulf between the strategic complexity of the market landscape and the strategic capacity of leaders. Rather than sharpening their strategic eye and developing the ability to recognize patterns and see the future unfold in slow motion, leaders often muddle through this frenetic environment with reactive, one-off thinking (corporate whack-a-mole) or by running faster on the operational treadmill.

As a result, given the dearth of senior leaders who have the capacity to lead with big ideas that unlock new vistas of possibility and growth, aspiring strategic leaders lack a frame of reference for being strategic. As these highflyers ascend within the organization, they learn how to fight increasingly bigger fires, and solve increasingly complex problems, leaving few opportunities to develop the capacity to think and lead strategically in dynamic market environments undergoing profound change.

Two dimensions of organizational renewal and longevity

The infinity loop shown in Figure 2 illustrates that there is an organizational dimension and a strategic dimension to renewal.

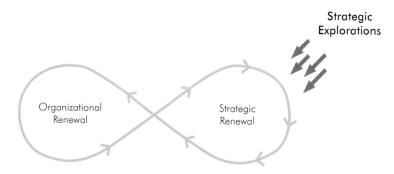

Figure 2

Organizationally, firms have made great strides over the past several decades in turbocharging hidebound hierarchies so that they are more adaptive and responsive to market changes. Through a steady stream of organizational innovations, such as autonomous teams, lean start-up, high-velocity decision making, hackathons, honeycombed organizational structures, ambidexterity, agile, and new business accelerators, firms have become flatter, fitter, and fleeter.

To foster emergence and autopoiesis (self-renewal), companies are increasingly taking cues from nature and abandoning top-down management principles and hierarchical structures in favor of organizational designs, processes, and cultures that embody the dynamic properties of ecosystems, such as a rainforest. The Chinese multinational firm Haier is a prime example. Over the past four decades, it has undergone a remarkable metamorphosis, from a mainstream white goods manufacturer to its current incarnation as an ecosystem-based enterprise encompassing a labyrinth of interconnected businesses, from smart cities to education to health care. Through its self-organizing network of microenterprises and its propagation-based growth model, the firm draws on evolutionary principles to unleash the animal spirits of its employees and create an autopoietic enterprise that essentially mirrors the connectedness and dynamism of the external market.

Cutting-edge advances in organizational designs and methodologies play an important role in helping firms adapt and keep pace with their external environment, but they are internally focused and not designed for sensing subtle shifts in the external landscape that reshape existing markets and create new ones. This is where strategic explorations come into play.

Strategic explorations: Opening the aperture to avoid a Kodak moment

> *There was nothing to turn around to.*
> — *Antonio Pérez, former Kodak CEO*

When leading renewal efforts, executives tend to focus on what they can perceive with their five senses. The greatest obstacle to renewal, however, is invisible — the prevailing mental models (small-scale models of reality) and belief systems that harden over time, creating strategic myopia, an acute condition in which organizations look at the outside world through a peephole.

The imperative, therefore, is to keep the strategic aperture open by continually questioning, examining, and transforming prevailing mental models and belief systems—the strategic equivalent of apoptosis and biogenesis — so they are malleable and able to perceive and respond to subtle market shifts.

Many years ago, Peter Drucker spoke of the importance of *looking out the window to see what is visible, but not yet seen* [by others] — an aphorism for scanning the external market landscape to identify the signals, both weak and strong, that portend profound market shifts. As a rule, the more dynamic and uncertain the external environment, the more time a company needs to spend looking out the window and engaging in deep strategic reflection and dialogue to recognize intersecting trends and patterns that pose exogenous opportunities and threats.

Incredibly, as simple as it sounds, looking out the window is an unnatural act in many established firms. Sophisticated cognitive capabilities (divergent thinking, curiosity, imagination, pattern recognition, paradoxical thinking, framing strategic questions, reflection, and synthesis) are needed to engage in strategic sense-making activities — capabilities that are often lacking in operationally oriented managers. Further complicating matters are a host of organizational pathologies that function as an invisible hand, influencing what we see and how we see it.

However, with the right developmental journey and organizational environment, operationally oriented managers can escape the denominator management box and learn *how to look out the window* and think strategically about converging trends and patterns that shape and create markets. Central to this approach are immersive, multi-month strategic explorations in which a cohort of next-generation enterprise leaders explore broadly framed, board-level strategic questions and engage in strategic reflection and dialogue under the watchful eye of an expert facilitator (typically an external partner) to develop their strategic capacity and infuse new thinking into the organization. Working in partnership with the CEO, the facilitator plays an important role in creating a generative space for strategic questioning, reflection, and dialogue to occur. (Think Yoda from *Star Wars* in an Armani suit).

To illustrate, let's say you're an auto manufacturer like General Motors or Volkswagen. A board-level question would undoubtedly concern the concept of "peak car" (automobile) and how the growing preference for access to transportation (mobility-as-a-service) over ownership in many market segments will affect the century-old business model of making and selling cars to customers who prefer to purchase, maintain, and drive their own vehicles. Participants begin by immersing themselves in the tangle of socioeconomic, technological, and environmental trends that are shaping the emerging mobility landscape, honing their skills in spotting emerging trends that foretell fundamental market shifts, before making their way to business model and organizational implications.

Strategic leaders think in the form of questions; framing strategic questions to stimulate reflection and dialogue is an important leadership competency and sense-making tool in complex market environments. Sadly, this has become a lost art in today's execution-oriented organizations, especially among high-strung leaders who pride themselves on having all the answers. This is where the external facilitator comes into play. Using Socratic inquiry, the facilitator (Yoda) poses penetrating, often unsettling, questions at key moments to unlock the shackles of short-termism and incrementalism and provoke deeper levels of strategic thinking: *What are potential future scenarios concerning vehicle ownership versus mobility-as-a-service? How will traditional industry boundaries likely evolve? Will they blur and converge into entirely new market arenas? What will be your core business ten years from now and how will value be created? How quickly will the future arrive? What signposts do you need to monitor?*

At regular intervals, the facilitator leads unscripted sessions with the cohort and the CEO to hone participants' strategic thinking and dialogue skills. Gradually, through successive rounds of question framing, reflection, and dialogue, participants master the language, logic, and lens of strategic leadership. Later in the exploration, as a point of view coalesces concerning the shifting contours of the mobility landscape, unstructured strategic dialogue sessions are held with the executive team, and, eventually, the board, to shape the strategic narrative and build systems-level strategic capacity.

Strategic explorations can be used in any organizational context but are particularly effective in companies facing increasing competitive intensity and market dynamism, or that are approaching an inflection point, such as the oil and gas industry, which is facing a peak demand scenario as clean energy sources gain ground. They can be launched periodically throughout the year to keep the organizational aperture open and fresh thinking flowing into the enterprise. I have guided scores of teams over the years and am always impressed by the quality of thinking and dialogue, as well as the generative power of these explorations in shifting executive worldviews and imbuing new perspectives and possibilities.

This is just the opening act

The past 25 years have been a tumultuous time for incumbents, especially those who have amassed their fortunes within stable oligopolies.

In the coming decade, rapid adoption of artificial intelligence, robotics, blockchain, additive manufacturing (3D printing), and the Internet of Things will spin the flywheel ever faster. The collision of the exponential growth curves of the Digital Age (think Alibaba and Airbnb) and the linear S-curves of the Industrial Era will likely shorten corporate life spans even further.

A pond will quickly become stagnant without a fresh source of water. The same can be said for organizations. A steady flow of new questions, conversations, and perspectives are needed to keep an organization's aperture open and its mental models and belief systems from becoming stagnant and out of sync with market realities. Strategic explorations are the revitalizing fountain that enable established firms to maintain their youth.

About the author

Dr. Jeffrey Kuhn is an executive advisor and educator focused on enterprise strategy, leadership, and transformation. His work centers on helping senior business leaders develop the capacity to think and lead strategically in dynamic market environments undergoing profound change. He holds a doctorate in adult and organizational learning from Columbia University.

Developing a transformational culture

DAVID LIDDLE

10

Imagine working in an organization with a clearly defined purpose and set of core values which connect us with our organization, with one another, and with our customers. Where our leaders are committed to unlocking our inner brilliance and engaging with each of us as human beings — during the good times and the bad. Where each voice is heard, each contribution is valued, and our differences are a source of celebration.

Imagine our organizations where our managers value and nature our happiness, our health and our harmony. Where mistakes become opportunities to learn and grow, and where failure becomes a catalyst for insight and innovation.

Imagine our organizations thriving and growing, where boardroom executives listen and respond to the needs of our diverse stakeholders. Where investments can be made safe in the knowledge that our organizations will act responsibly and justly. Where profit and integrity go hand and hand, and where corruption, exploitation and abuse of power are challenged and resolved through fair, transparent and robust systems of governance and accountability.

Imagine all of this in an organization which recognizes it has a responsibility to our planet, and which works hard to protect the rich and diverse ecosystems within which we all live, play and work.

At a time when organizations are straining every sinew to build back better following some of the most turbulent times in the last 20 years, it is becoming increasingly clear that it is not possible to emerge with the old cultural paradigms still in play. Power, profit and process are no longer symbols of a successful organization.

If we are to build the kind of organizations imagined at the beginning of this chapter, we need a new form of organizational culture — a transformational culture which will allow organizations to continually adapt, transform and grow as they deal with the pressing challenges of today — and others that may yet be around the corner as we gradually emerge from the COVID-19 pandemic.

A new cultural paradigm

Culture is the greatest asset, or the greatest liability, an organization has. Yet, for so many, culture is barely talked about and it is the only asset, or liability, that no one has direct ownership of. It is widely misunderstood, routinely ignored; yet a potential source of riches when it is managed well.

As an asset, good company culture can drive employee experience and engender trust and respect. It can create safe and healthy workplaces and ensure customers, investors and stakeholders receive the very best that the company has to offer. In a good culture, customers and employees are naturally inclined to spread the good word and become an advocate and supporter for what you do. Conversely, when cultures go wrong, they can become a liability. They can be stifling, toxic, dysfunctional, destructive, corrosive, divisive, fear-inducing and unsafe places to work within, or to do business with.

Current cultural orthodoxies are not working, are no longer fit for purpose and are unravelling before our very eyes. We can either leave the development of our organizational culture to chance, or we can actively develop the culture in a way which ensures our organizations will be competitive and sustainable long into the future. The smart investors, the smart candidates, and the smart customers will choose the latter.

What is a transformational culture?

A transformational culture is an organizational culture which is fair, just, inclusive, sustainable and high performing. It offers a new cultural paradigm and a practical framework for organizations which are committed to putting their purpose, their people and their values first.

A transformational culture is suitable for organizations of any size and in any sector, bound by a common purpose to develop a workplace where the success of the organization and the success of its employees, customers and stakeholders are inextricably aligned.

In a transformational culture, the HR systems and management processes which promulgate mistrust, fear, injustice, exclusion, blame and retribution are supplanted with new systems and new processes which institutionalize trust, fairness, learning, growth, dialogue, inclusion, insight and collaboration. This new form of organizational culture requires a significant shift in focus and emphasis. But the rewards will be great, measured in terms of enhanced competitive advantage, attracting investment, enhanced brand values and the ability to attract and retain top talent.

The Transformational Triangle™

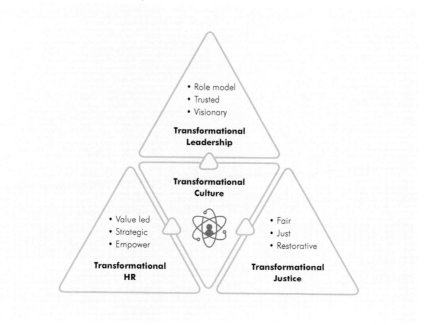

What does a transformational culture look like in practice?

The Transformational Triangle model above represents the three elements of a transformational culture: transformational HR, transformational leadership and transformational justice. These three elements work in harmony to influence the development of a transformational culture.

Transformational Leadership: The transformational leader demonstrates an alignment of their behavior with the purpose and values of the organization. They know it is important to walk the talk, because they understand that they are a role model — that the way they behave sets the tone for the culture of their organization. Moreover, it defines the climate and the terms of engagement (the micro-culture) within their teams, divisions and departments. Transformational leaders and managers act with courage and kindness. They listen actively, they respond constructively, and they lead with integrity. Within a transformational culture, leaders and managers possess the courage, the confidence and the competence to spot and resolve concerns, conflicts and complaints constructively. Leaders and managers must also be empowered to take action to resolve issues at work rather than subcontracting problems to the HR function, or relying on the popular management norms of extensive inaction or expensive overreaction.

Transformational Justice: A transformational culture is also about enabling a radical shift in the way that our organizations think about justice. Justice is at the heart of a civilized society, but the question begs to be asked: do our organization's rules, procedures and policies deliver justice? I would suggest not. Transformational justice is a new model of justice which balances the rules of the organization, the rights of the employee, and the need to generate fair, just and inclusive outcomes when things go wrong. At its core, it is about reducing harm, building trust, protecting relationships, promoting psychological safety and creating opportunities for insight, reflection and learning. Transformational justice replaces the retributive models of justice which are deeply ingrained throughout organizational processes such as the traditional performance management, discipline and grievance procedures. These retributive justice processes are concerned about risk mitigation, blame and punishment. They are harmful, damaging and divisive — and worse still, their sheer existence invokes an adversarial and confrontational mindset and dynamic in teams, departments, divisions and across entire organizations.

Transformational HR: If organizations are going to adopt a transformational culture, the human resources function must take urgent action to become purpose, people and values led. HR must transform itself into an overarching people and culture function and it should act now to release itself from the burden of its perceived proximity to management. The term 'business partner,' so casually used, is a divisive and loaded term which results in HR being perceived by many as the 'long arm of management.' This perception of systemic bias impedes the effectiveness of HR and it erodes trust in its role and its systems. For HR to remain a trusted and effective function in our organizations, it must rise above the paradigms of power, hierarchy and control. It must become obsessed with delivering great employee experience (EX) and becoming a catalyst for world-class customer experience (CX). HR should be the function within our organizations that connects EX with CX.

The Transformational Culture Model

To assist with this transformation, I have created a powerful organizational change model, which is set out below.

The Transformational Culture Model™

The Transformational Culture Model offers a blueprint for a progressive, values-based and people-centered organization. It is a blend of interconnected elements which span an organization's entire ecosystem. The model can be used to support the process of designing, deploying and sustaining the necessary changes which will deliver a fair, just, inclusive, sustainable and high-performance organizational culture. The application of the model is supported through enhanced people processes, management systems and leadership strategies and behaviors. While offering a cultural framework, it is not prescriptive. The model is designed to adapt and flex to meet the organization's unique sector, maturity, context, geography, needs and circumstances.

The Transformational Culture Model comprises three core elements:

1. The Transformational Culture Hub: this is the cross-functional body which supports the design, deployment and evaluation of the transformational culture.
2. The eight enablers of a transformational culture: these are the elements which drive and sustain a transformational culture.
3. The measurable impact of a transformational culture: these are the 7Cs which result from a transformational culture. They also provide the fuel to turbo charge its integration across your organization.

A detailed description of the role of the hub and 7Cs can be found in my book *Transformational Culture*.[50]

In this article, we look in detail at the eight enablers of a transformational culture. The eight enablers are the central part of the Transformational Culture Model and operate together to form a whole system.

Enabler 1: Values First

Values are the golden thread that runs through an organization. They bind a transformational culture together by aligning an organization's purpose and strategy with its agreed behaviors and the overall customer and employee experience. Your values should reflect the kind of organization you are and the kind of organization you want to be. In other words, whether written or unwritten, the values of your organization are perhaps one of its most valuable commodities and they should be authentic and aspirational.

To define an organization's values, one first needs to be clear about its purpose. The purpose of your organization defines the reason it exists. Leaders need to think hard about how to make purpose central to their strategy. Avoid generic-sounding purposes such as 'making the world better' or 'delivering excellence' as these are meaningless and increase suspicion that this is a corporate PR exercise.

Purpose and values provide a solid foundation to the organization's employee value proposition (EVP). They act as a glue which galvanizes and motivates the workforce and they provide a pivot point around which changes are delivered.

Enabler 2: Evidence Based

The use of data and evidence to inform and evaluate a program of cultural change is central to its short and long term success. Without the evidence base, and the necessary data to help us plan, it is like embarking on a journey in the dead of night, in someone else's car, not knowing where you are going, without a map and with a phone which we forgot to charge. To ensure that it has maximum impact, and can be sustained, the design and deployment of a transformational culture requires an evidence-based approach from inception.

People and culture professionals (HR), managers, leaders, employees, unions and other stakeholders generate an incredible amount of management information, much of which can be applied to a process of cultural transformation. The data gathered as part of developing a transformational culture can be used to support the development of a business case, to identify gaps, hotspots, trends and patterns in the business and to provide valuable baseline data, against which the impact of the cultural changes can be evaluated over the short, medium and long term.

Enabler 3: The People and Culture Function

Continually evolving and adapting, the HR profession is perhaps one of the most transformative of all organizational functions. The ever-changing legal landscape, digitalization and globalization, coupled with continuous pressure from leaders to recruit and retain top talent and achieve more from their 'human capital' has placed greater and greater pressure on the modern HR professional.

As organizations strive to build back better, HR yet again stands at a crossroads. The existing HR orthodoxies are being challenged and the meaning of HR is being hotly debated. HR policies and procedures, which once seemed so solid and reliable, are now being shown to be retributive, damaging and destructive. HR's ability to deliver strategic value and to attract and retain talent is being weakened by persistently low levels of employee engagement and productivity, increasing levels of employee activism and rising levels of inequality. HR needs to adapt quickly to this new reality and must reject the dogmas and orthodoxies which have acted as a drag on the potential of the HR function for too many years.

Enabler 4: Leadership and Management

Our leaders are integral to the nature of the organizational culture and managers are integral to the climate within a team or department. The way in which a leader or manager behaves is perhaps the single biggest factor affecting organizational culture and climate. The way that our CEOs, executives and managers behave creates the unwritten cues and clues for the rest of the workforce. Many managers and leaders do not realize that through their actions, interactions and reactions (AIR), they are shaping the climate of their teams and the culture of their organization. A transformational culture offers them a new set of cultural norms within which they can choose to behave and by which they can be held to account for the choices that they make.

Enabler 5: The Resolution Framework

The Resolution Framework[51] epitomizes transformational justice. It replaces an organization's retributive justice systems, including performance, discipline and grievance procedures, with a single, fully integrated structure for handling and resolving concerns, conduct, complaints and conflicts.

The Resolution Framework comprises several elements which make it a highly effective policy in a contemporary and progressive employee handbook:

- It is values based and person centered.
- Dialogue has primacy.
- Retributive justice has been replaced. Restorative justice and procedural justice have been combined to create a powerful model of transformational justice.
- A new triage process and resolution index are used for assessing the most appropriate route to resolution in each case.
- There is increased use of restorative justice processes, such as facilitation, mediation, coaching and team conferences.

Enabler 6: Well-being, Engagement and Inclusion

Employee well-being, engagement and inclusion are now so interwoven and so interconnected that I believe they should now be considered as a single discipline. These three elements are central to overall EX and as a result they hold the key to delivering great CX. I have been involved in the areas of well-being, engagement and inclusion all my working life. I have seen policies, strategies and programs come and go, yet the ability to deliver a happy, healthy and harmonious workforce still eludes a great many organizations.

Why is this? One of the key issues is that the systematic failure by a great many organizations to treat conflict as a strategic priority is a direct cause of low engagement, poor mental health and exclusion at work. Engagement programs, well-being initiatives, HR procedures and zero tolerance policies will not work until the issue of how we handle differences, disputes and dissent effectively is resolved. The irony is that the processes and the initiatives that our organizations deploy exacerbate stress, worsen fear and deepen anxiety. These major issues which can be resolved by implementing a transformational culture and by aligning well-being, engagement and inclusion.

Enabler 7: Sustainability and Social Justice

Sustainability and social justice are pressures which have barely appeared on the risk register of most organizations. Virtually overnight, that has all changed — to the extent that these two imperatives will become the defining characteristics of the 21st century.

The pressure on organizations to respond to the threats of climate change is great. In an attempt to secure a position of leadership in the area of climate action, more and more investors are investing in companies which are working to achieve net zero carbon emissions and are committed to environment, social and corporate governance (ESG).

Social justice and the development of an inclusive economy is another imperative which has moved off the streets and into our boardrooms and offices. Historically, our workplace cultures have been influenced by forces from within the organization or from a well-managed group of external stakeholders. However, through long-term lockdowns we saw a profound shift in society in terms of expectations around justice (witness the Black Lives Matter and #MeToo movements).

The widespread reorientation of the employee's relationship with the employer, and with society at large, is profoundly changing company culture. The successful CEOs and executives will recognize that the culture of their organizations must align with the growing wave of employee and social activism, whether that comes from within or without.

Enabler 8: Brand, Reputation and Risk

Open any newspaper or visit any newsfeed and it is plain to see that the culture of our organizations, the behavior of our leaders and the way we treat our employees have a significant impact on the reputation of our companies. Reputation is based on the behaviors, competencies, values and communications exhibited by a company. As Ed Coke, director at Repute Associates in London explains, if organizations underperform against expectation in any one of these areas, the ultimate outcome — the trust that stakeholders place in a company — can be compromised.

The relationship between leadership and culture is central to an organization's brand and reputation. It follows therefore that clarity, consistency and appropriateness of communication have important roles to play in employees' and stakeholders' assessments of leadership. Taking each of these attributes of leadership and codifying them, whether formally or informally, within a workplace, and — critically — actively and consistently demonstrating these attributes, establishes company culture.

At this time of great uncertainty, and with the need for something solid and tangible to work with, the Transformational Culture Model and the eight enablers of a transformational culture offer a flexible blueprint for a modern and progressive organization. But for it to deliver maximum and sustained impact, the model requires fresh thinking on the part of our leaders, managers, unions and other key stakeholders. This is a model that drives a new mindset, a new working paradigm and a new set of behaviors. It requires courage and a commitment to change. Rising above the challenges that are being thrust upon us, whether they are coming from COVID-19, the resulting economic shock, geopolitical changes, or social and employee activism, will require our organizations to be ever more fleet of foot, predictive and proactive.

About the author

David Liddle is CEO of the transformational culture consultancy, The TCM Group and founding president of the Institute of Organizational Dynamics. He is the author of two books *Managing Conflict* (Kogan Page/CIPD) and *Transformational Culture: Develop a People-Centred Organization for Improved Performance* (Kogan Page, 2021).

Footnotes

50 David Liddle, *Transformational Culture*, Kogan Page, 2021.

51 Liddle, D. (2021) The Resolution Framework. A fully integrated approach for resolving concerns, complaints and conflicts at work, www.resolutionframework.com

Organizing for perpetual transformation

HABEEB MAHABOOB

11

Globalization, digitization, and access to capital are leading organizations to operate at a much larger scale and speed than ever before. Companies cannot remain successful if they continue to work as they have for generations. In the past, organizational transformations were rare, and when they did occur, it was a long, drawn-out process. But organizations are now in a state of perpetual transformation.

Ongoing transformation has become a necessity rather than an option. Most of the successful organizations we see today, irrespective of their industry, have adapted and evolved over the years. To stay relevant, these organizations identified newer opportunities and leveraged them for survival, growth, and success.

While the word transformation has been overused in recent years, it is probably the only word that adequately describes the large-scale, identity-defining change that happens within an organization. The objective of a transformation is sustained value creation based on an understanding of evolving stakeholder context, internal capabilities and customer needs.

One company that has come to epitomize sustained transformation is Netflix. Since its inception, the company has undergone significant and multiple transformations by anticipating customer needs to become the behemoth it is now. Netflix transformed its business model from a DVD rental business to a pay-for-use model to a subscription model. Despite its massive successes, Netflix continues to experiment and flourish. The company's relentless initiatives are part of the organizational transformation it is perpetually going through.

Past approaches to transformation

The infrequency of transformations in the past meant that organizing for transformation was sporadic and at best projectized. Firms tended to transform themselves by changing hard factors like processes, operating models, organizational structures; or soft factors like people and culture; or some combination of both.

A number of transformational tools and frameworks became popular. The *lean transformation model* is an example of an approach aimed at continuous process improvement, with a focus on eliminating waste. Organizations following this model used a set of dedicated individuals (often called Master Black Belts) and part-time resources to deliver transformation through a series of projects. Mature organizations also tied these projects to the strategic goals of the organization.

The *ADKAR model* (short for awareness, desire, knowledge, ability, and reinforcement) is a soft skills or people-oriented approach to develop individuals and improve the chances of transformation at an organizational level. Harvard professor John Kotter's *8-Step Process for Leading Change*, gave an outline to implement change systematically and effectively.

While these approaches certainly have their merits, they don't suit the challenges of continuous transformation now facing organizations, in which ambiguity, speed, agility, and resilience are of paramount importance.[52] Hence there must be a fundamental shift in the transformational approaches adopted by organizations and a change in the entities tasked with leading the transformation journey. Organizations need to pursue perpetual transformation and adopt tools that make it achievable.

Considerations for organizing for perpetual transformation

The disruptions that we are witnessing today are unlike anything we have seen in the past. The three distinguishing factors of present-day changes are:

- **Speed:** value chains undergoing rapid and fundamental shifts both from within and from outside.
- **Technology:** rapid advances along with improved capabilities in big data, analytics, infrastructure, and other technologies, such as artificial intelligence, have removed the barriers that traditionally existed between industries.
- **New players:** markets are witnessing the introduction of new entrants or organizations from other industries.

As firms organize for perpetual transformation, the structures they adopt need to address the above factors. More importantly, these transformational structures or entities also need to be a permanent part of the organization, rather than temporary for a limited time. In its consulting work, our firm (BE Tech Mahindra) uses the following framework and recommends these organizational structures to ensure ongoing successful evolution.[53]

Perpetual Transformation Framework

Organizations setting themselves up for ongoing evolution need to consider the following activities/organizational elements to enable the transformation:

1. **Explore and Identify:** organizations can engage experts who continuously analyze the environment by scanning, discovering, and assimilating opportunities. These experts can be drawn from the internal talent pool or from external resources, such as professional consultants, subject matter experts, or a mix of both. These listening/scanning posts ideally need to be in geographical hotspots of innovation in their respective sector/domain. Using academics who connect and open innovation (through hackathons and the like) are also ways in which organizations can develop a pipeline of ideas that will impact their businesses.

2. **Evaluate and Incubate:** our studies indicate that incubation of ideas within a firm is a key failure point. This typically stems from an inability to identify specific individuals or teams to own new ideas within the business. Even when identified, the ability of the owners to prioritize incubation activities over running the ongoing business is often poor. Some organizations adopt the mergers and acquisitions route to gain new capabilities or use the acquired companies as an incubator for testing new business ideas. Identifying and dedicating the right talent to incubate an idea (or transformation goal) within the company is the next crucial phase of a transformation journey.

3. **Implement and Scale:** implementation of transformation actions is the next crucial aspect of success. While we have yet to find a formula for successful transformation, being able to establish a (project) management organization, convert transformation goals to manageable projects, drive multiple levers of transformation in an integrated manner, and energize the company through a sustained communication and risk/reward program are some of the essential activities for success at this stage.

Managing perpetual transformation

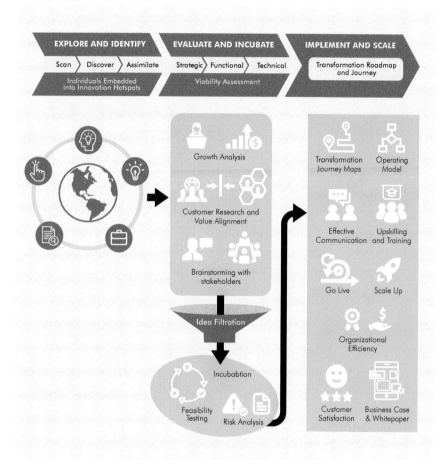

Managing perpetual transformation

Given that transformation is now continuous and has no end point, organizations need to consider the following factors when designing their operating model to drive transformation:

- Transformations can no longer be projectized as they once were.
- Successful transformations still need to address multiple levers, including people, processes, operating models, and the business model.
- Transformation goals will be achieved in increments rather than all at once.
- Organization-wide involvement is required to ensure successful transformation.

Based on the above, organizations need to find appropriate answers to the following four questions to ensure achievement of transformation goals on an ongoing basis:

1. Do we need a Chief Transformation Officer?

Traditionally, organizations have assigned responsibility for transformation to one or more senior operational unit leaders in the firm. Operational business leaders have struggled to dedicate mindshare and time to drive transformation. Given the ongoing nature of the role now, firms may need to appoint someone with dedicated and clear mandate to drive change. The demerit of this approach is that operating units disown accountability within their units.

The other alternative is for the CEO to take up the responsibility for driving waves of transformation. This approach may allow the CEO to balance the day-to-day needs of the business with the need for change. However, the CEO may require support to execute the transformation agenda. For this reason, organizations would be advised to formalize the role of a Chief Transformation Officer.[54] The seniority and location of the role are decisions that should be based on the unique circumstances of the organization. A well thought through strategy will identify which elements of the transformation need to be driven centrally and should guide the role and selection.

2. Do we need to staff a full-time transformation management office (TMO)?

Multiple studies have indicated that integrated transformation efforts that address multiple levers within the organization stand a higher chance of success. The role of an organizational entity responsible to strategize, plan, coordinate, and report progress on transformation on an ongoing basis becomes vital in this context.[55]

Our studies indicate that TMOSs (like any staff function) fall into one of three design patterns as detailed below:[56]

- **Weather stations:** weather station TMOs tend to focus on providing the organization with feedback on the status of the transformation. Typically staffed by analysts, the TMO focuses on collecting, integrating, and presenting progress reports. The actual tasks associated with the transformation are the responsibility of the various operational entities.

- **Coaches:** organizations which recognize the importance of capability building as an enabler of successful transformation provide TMOs, which guide and coach transformation teams. Formal training and certification programs are introduced under the guidance of the TMO to build a network of change agents. The TMO will also have senior change leaders who are able to work with work stream leaders to coach and mentor them to address the ongoing challenges they face. This is the preferred model for TMOs, given the ongoing evolution of work streams that are part of any perpetual transformation.
- **Control towers:** A few organizations find merit in establishing powerful TMOs with accountability to achieve transformation results. Control tower TMOs have accountability for these goals and in many cases authority to override functional units on approach and decisions related to transformation.

Irrespective of the role of the transformation office, organizations need to visualize transformations — not as long duration projects, but as a series of incremental releases, each delivering specific business benefits. Organizations also need to ensure that TMOs are staffed with adequate communication capabilities to articulate and energize the entire organization around ongoing change.

3. Do we need any additional organizational entities to support scanning and incubation?

Another key factor to consider for ongoing transformation is establishing the entities tasked with bringing new ideas into the organization. Traditionally, R&D and marketing functions have played this role. Organizations are advised to strengthen these functions, and to evaluate their ways of working including association with academic organizations and partners developing cutting-edge technologies. The physical location of these units — close to innovation hotspots — is an important consideration.

4. Do we need change agents to embed change in operational units?

While the elements discussed above will act as enablers, real change happens within the operational units of the firm. It is important that organizations provide sufficient capacity (slack) within operational units to drive change.

In the future, organizations will rely on being in a state of perpetual transformation for continuous value creation. With a deep understanding of the internal and external environment, organizations should organize for ongoing transformation, while being mindful of their culture and unique capabilities.

About the author

Habeeb Mahaboob is a managing consultant with BE, the consulting and management services division of Tech Mahindra. Tech Mahindra offers innovative and customer-centric digital experiences, enabling enterprises, associates, and the society to rise. Habeeb brings expertise in working with businesses to articulate the impact of digital technologies (through top-down analysis of the firm from an industry, market, and end customer perspective or through facilitated design thinking-based workshops) and in working with client teams to conceptualize new operating models to achieve digital goals. Habeeb has worked closely with multiple clients to effectively lead the digital agenda of their respective firms.

Habeeb's colleagues from the India office, Alex Francis Komban, Himanshu Yadav, Sanjeevan Palit, and Abhay Agrawal co-authored the article. Abhishek Anand closely works with PMI in developing these concepts.

Footnotes

52 https://www.linkedin.com/pulse/leading-perpetual-change-will-duke

53 Oliver Bossert and Jürgen Laartz, Perpetual evolution--the management approach required for digital transformation', McKinsey Digital, 5 June 2017.

54 'The Chief Transformation Officer Role Explained', BMC Software Blogs.

55 'The role of the transformation office', McKinsey Online.

56 'Choose the right type of PMO for your business model', ITM Platform.

The transformation office as a permanent part of organizational life

REINHARD MESSENBOECK, KRISTY
ELLMER, DAVID KIRCHHOFF, MIKE LEWIS,
PERRY KEENAN, SIMON STOLBA AND
CONNOR CURRIER

12

Transformations are critical to delivering stakeholder value and competitive advantage — especially in fast-changing industries. Yet Boston Consulting Group's analysis of data from more than 3,000 transformations shows that the vast majority of transformations (more than 70 percent) fail. While the failure rate has worsened during the pandemic, it has been appallingly high for many years. This is no surprise: transformations are inherently difficult. Their goals typically include significant shifts in operational processes, product offerings, governance, structure, and most importantly in the way people behave. They call for a step-change improvement in performance, which typically requires new ways of working and a deeper understanding of customers.

Because of the pace of change in business and the need for near-constant adaptations, some companies have embraced the idea of the perpetual or "always-on" transformation. This is different in two ways from the continuous improvement initiatives that many companies engage in. First, while continuous improvement initiatives are generally bottom-up, always-on transformations are typically top down. The second difference has to do with ambition. Unlike continuous improvement, an always-on transformation isn't about incremental changes. It targets the "big rocks" that — once moved — will lead to fundamental improvements in a company's prospects. Companies that embrace the idea of always-on transformation do so with the intention of creating significant changes on a sustained basis.

The Rhythms of an "Always-On" Transformation

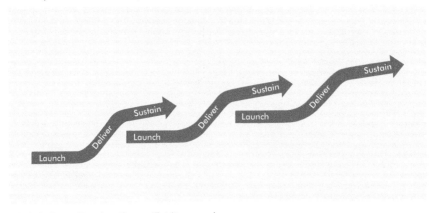

Every successful transformation — and certainly any successful always-on transformation — depends on the deft management of three journeys. There is a people journey, which has to do with maximizing employees' engagement. There is a leader journey, which has to do with the job of setting the initial goals and targets — and then raising the goals and setting new targets as a way to keep the organization advancing. And then there is the program journey — the focus of this article. It is about establishing a framework and a set of processes to maximize transparency, measurement and accountability.

The program journey is especially crucial for companies that are in a state of perpetual transformation. These are typically companies in fast-changing industries, that know each year's annual plan is going to rely on the achievement of three or four major new initiatives. When so much is riding on your ability to successfully make a few major changes, executional certainty becomes crucial. We believe that the best way to achieve such certainty is through two transformation elements:

1. A well-structured transformation office and
2. A robust stage-gate methodology.

1. What a properly structured transformation office looks like

A successful transformation depends on the collective willingness of people to do things differently. For change to stick and initiatives to be successfully executed, clear goals, consequences and accountability are all necessary. Ensuring that these are in place is the responsibility of the transformation office.

A truly great transformation goes beyond delivering hoped-for business goals and elevates the executional capability of the organization as a whole. In such a transformation, both leaders and everyday workers develop new capabilities.

The reason this is so hard — and that successful transformations are so rare — has to do with the human side of organizations. At an individual level, the very idea of change creates a lot of internal conflict for people. Behavioral scientists have names for these conflicts:

- The intention-action gap — people's tendency to not do what they say, and sometimes to not even do what they intend to do
- Loss aversion — the phenomenon of fearing failure more than one seeks success
- The status quo bias — people's tendency to favor the known over the new.

One or another of these behavioral norms exist in all of us to some degree — and they are among the impediments in every transformation. They likely explain one of the most common complaints in transformations, of the leader who isn't committed or isn't taking the transformation seriously. Everybody is counting on the leader to deliver something, and it's not getting done.

On top of the problems of individual adjustment and acceptance, there are often a host of top-down problems in transformations, mostly around two fundamental issues: the desired behaviors not being clearly articulated (so people don't know what is expected) or the business context in which people operate not reinforcing these desired behaviors.

And of course, there is always the possibility of plain old inertia — of people simply not being able to get started. A framework we call ATAC can help with behavior activation. ATAC includes:

- **Anchoring**, the discipline of keeping the organization focused on the main objectives and ambitions of the transformation. Anchoring requires some kind of metric — often financial in nature. Good transformation offices continually ask about the achievement of these metrics. That ensures that the rest of the organization gets the message.
- **Transparency** is essential if desired behaviors, in keeping with the main transformation objectives, are to be encouraged. Transparency implies visibility throughout an organization, including into the organization's lower levels. Organization-wide transparency can be achieved in many ways, including through dashboards, checklists and personal check-ins.
- **Accountability** refers to the need to make each individual accountable for their own expected behaviors throughout the transformation.
- **Consequences** are needed to keep the transformation on track. Consequences include management support and performance coaching when goals are unmet or when a staff member underperforms. Consequences can also be positive — the celebration of success either verbally or through tangible rewards.

The transformation office's mechanisms for supporting change activities aren't , on their face, revolutionary. A lot of it consists of meetings, decision-making routines, the use of tracking protocols and an insistence on transparency. But the discipline with which a good transformation office does all of this can create a powerful impetus for new behaviors and can set the stage for success whether a transformation is "one and done" or ongoing.

Routines and tracking. Transformations are never glitch-free. Even in a well-run program, 20 percent of initiatives won't achieve their desired impact; even more initiatives (30 percent) will typically be at risk. In fact, if too many initiatives in a transformation are seen as easily achieved, leadership probably hasn't been ambitious enough in setting goals.

Rigorously defined milestones and metrics are a cornerstone of any transformation. In regularly scheduled meetings — once a week, or once every two weeks — the transformation office brings together each operating unit or function to discuss the status of its initiatives, projects, and milestones. This creates opportunities for agile problem solving and for pivots that are critical for maintaining momentum and reaching key targets.

As the head of this crucial group, the job of the chief transformation officer (CTO) is to break down silos and get the organization to work together. This happens in meetings in which people from operations, finance, production, marketing and other departments are brought together. Finally, the transformation office hosts weekly meetings of the steering committee (SteerCo), which is the group that oversees the program's progress and makes decisions that no other body can make. It is critical that the ultimate owner or "sponsor" of the program (usually the CEO, CFO, or other top leader) attend the weekly Steerco meetings. By doing so, he or she sends a message about the importance of the transformation and of all transformation-related activities.

During a typical week, the transformation office maintains an intense meeting cadence — and that's by design. A transformation isn't business as usual and shouldn't feel like business as usual. The degree of transparency, accountability and cross-functional cooperation that transformations require is not how organizations function naturally. At least initially, the program should make the people involved feel a little uncomfortable. Initiative owners and milestone owners need to know they're being counted on to make progress every day and they should also know, when one week's meeting ends, what they need to achieve before the next week's meeting. At the same time, the meetings are a chance to identify and remove roadblocks. This often means decisions and follow-up actions for higher-level executives. Indeed, transformations often "flip the pyramid," forcing executives to solve problems for people one, two, or three levels down from them. "Nowhere to run, nowhere to hide, and no one to blame but yourself," is the way one executive put it to us, at a point where he was just starting to understand what his company's transformation would require of him.

It's a little bit like what happens when you sign on with a personal trainer for the first time. Initially, the workouts seem beyond your ability and it's frustrating. With progress, however, comes confidence and greater trust in the process.

Effective transformation offices follow three meeting best practices:

- **They focus on cross-department problem-solving.** In a transformation, the top opportunities inevitably require cooperation across functional boundaries. A good transformation office helps different functions understand what they have to gain by collaborating. This emphasis on what's optimal for all increases managers' trust in the transformation office and allows the CTO to emerge as one of the leaders of the organization.
- **They have a bias toward working sessions.** "They're killing us with all these meetings" is a common complaint in organizations, and the risk that people will feel this way increases during transformations with all the new touchpoints that are required. A transformation office can eliminate some of this feeling by making it clear that the centerpiece of most meetings will be a centralized data system, containing the status of milestones and other important data — not newly created PowerPoint decks. Indeed, what the weekly meetings will consist of should be the topic of an initial meeting, prior to each meeting series, that allows the transformation's special terminology and likely rhythms to be discussed.
- **They create time for "uplift."** The transformation office should devote portions of some of its meetings to more personal interactions. An example of this is a daily "uplift" or moment to recognize a key accomplishment that has been driven either organizationally or by a specific member of a project team. The uplift moment can be short and simple, done with the understanding of the many ways that the celebration of small successes can inspire.

2. Creating a robust stage-gate methodology in perpetual transformations

From idea to execution — that's the path that every transformation follows. But no transformation has just one idea and one execution challenge. Instead, each transformation (and certainly every perpetual transformation) contains a constantly expanding set of ideas. The only way to manage them all is to systematize the effort. This is where stage gates come in.

Companies often downplay the value of stage gates, thinking they're a bureaucratic imposition that slows things down. In fact, a good stage-gate process (as in the diagram below) speeds things up and keeps them on course.

To show how stage gate works, we'll use the example of a household goods

The Elements of a Stage Gate Approach

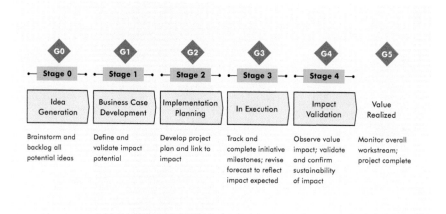

company whose transformation is aimed at increasing profit through digitization and customer centricity. One of the company's initiatives is to handle the sale of frequently reordered supplies exclusively through its online channel. To help deliver this initiative, the company has launched a project to ramp up its online pricing capability and offer discounts on online supplies during a transition period when both online and offline sales channels are still being used.

There's a core project team consisting of a product manager, the director of marketing, a regional retail liaison, an analyst from finance and a VP of web development. At the idea generation stage, the team would outline the idea and describe its benefits in a project charter — a short description of the goal and how it will be achieved. Stage 1 would be about validating the business case — namely, the ROI of the project itself and the eventual increase in per-unit profitability. If the project charter and business case withstand scrutiny, then the key milestones of the project plan (Stage 2) are developed including the location, length and goals of any pilot. If the project passes muster in Stages 1 and 2, it enters Stage 3 — execution. In Stage 4, the project is reviewed to determine if all its goals have been achieved.

Each stage plays an important role in strengthening the project. By the time it gets to Stage 3, a project that started out as a loose idea ideally should be reborn as an airtight plan.

The "gates" also contribute to the improvement process. At each gate, a group with a clear stake in the outcome looks at the work that the project team is doing and decides if the project is ready to move to the next stage. The first person with go/no-go authority at a gate is the business unit leader. There is also often another functional executive weighing in (maybe the head of sales in this example). The transformation office plays a key role in facilitating the movement of projects and initiatives across stages and ensuring that the transformation machinery is working efficiently.

While setting up a stage-gate program involves significant early work, it provides multiple benefits that ultimately allow the overall transformation to run smoothly and deliver full value. Among the benefits:

- Stage gate puts all ideas on a level playing field. The vetting process ensures prioritization of initiatives, ROI rigor and smart execution plans with clear milestones before projects and initiatives move into execution.
- The execution phase (Stage 3) puts projects into active weekly tracking and monitoring which creates transparency and focus.
- Having an explicit phase for measuring value delivery (Stage 4) ensures discipline on achieving outcomes at the project, initiative and overall program level.
- The common language and process enables comparisons across the portfolio.

Some stage-gate best practices

A couple of best practices can make the stage-gate methodology more effective. In our experience, successful projects have well thought out milestones (Stage 3). To help ensure this, many of the clients we work with make use of something we call a rigor test, which is basically a discussion right before the execution stage that involves all of a project's key stakeholders. Those doing the rigor test take a fresh look at the project: at the achievability of its goals and milestones and how well understood its risks and interdependencies are. Rigor-test discussions are generally short — no more than an hour — but it is amazing how often they expose some critical flaw: a milestone that has not been assigned or a dependency that no one has considered. The rigor tests make it more likely that flaws will be addressed, allowing projects to move into the execution and other stages with much higher likelihoods of success.

Another best practice is not to allow projects to proceed without the finance department's explicit approval of the business case (Stage 2). Finance's job is to assess the project's profit, loss, one-time cost and cash impact, and to make sure the project aligns with broader corporate financial requirements. BCG experience and research (including the ongoing benchmarking study we run, called "The Transformation Check"[57]) shows that there is a strong correlation between validating a project's business case and the project's eventual success. Indeed, when such validation is done, the chances of a project or initiative succeeding is 40 percentage points higher than if it's not done.

During the stage-gate work, successful transformation leaders assess the key success factors of their projects. The process that allows them to do this (which we call "DICE" — Duration, Integrity, Commitment and Effort) zeroes in on four factors: the "duration" between crucial milestones (similar to the aforementioned rigor test); the "integrity" of the project team (including the extent to which the project team has the needed skills mix); the "commitment" of senior management and the broader team; and the amount of "effort," over and above team members' current commitments, that the project requires. Projects score on a continuum that ranges from "set up for success" to "in danger of failing." The DICE assessment can be used at any point that it seems useful to the chief transformation officer, to a business unit leader, or to the SteerCo to help determine if a given project/initiative is being set up for success and to intervene if not.

The use of stage gates should not be dreaded as a rigid methodology. In fact, companies can cut down on the number of stages as long as they make sure of three things, in this order:

- That each business idea or project is thoroughly vetted
- That the development of the new service or organizational change is effectively planned and managed; and
- That milestones and metrics are used to measure the project's success and identify emerging risks.

The COVID-19 pandemic has forced organizations to make dramatic adaptations in the last 18 months. It has also made organizations more aware of the inevitability of change. Some of the change triggers — like automation and climate change — are clear in origin. Others aren't and are perhaps beyond our ability to imagine today. To address the coming changes, known and not, organizations must develop a capability for reinvention.

Indeed, there may well be an advantage in the future to companies that operate according to the rigors of perpetual, always-on, transformation. You'll know these companies by their permanent transformation offices and by the appearance of their CTOs in financial filings alongside of CEOs, chief financial officers, and chief technology officers. The transformation office and the CTO will be key to getting leaders and everyday employees to carry out their own transformation journeys and to putting in place the program journey that will keep the destination always in sight.

About the authors

Reinhard Messenboeck is a Managing Director and Senior Partner at BCG and leads the Change Management topic globally.

Kristy Ellmer is a Managing Director and Partner at BCG and leads the Change Management topic in North America.

David Kirchhoff is a Managing Director and Partner at BCG and core member of BCG TURN, the firms' accelerated transformation and turnaround unit.

Mike Lewis is a Managing Director and Partner at BCG and is globally leading KEY by BCG, the firms' digital performance platform for transformations.

Perry Keenan is a Managing Director and Senior Partner at BCG and former global leader of the Change Management topic.

Simon Stolba is a Consultant at BCG specializing in Change Management and transformations.

Connor Currier is a Knowledge Expert at BCG and is leading BCG's Change Management knowledge team globally.

Footnotes

57 Organizations interested in seeing how their transformations stack up can access BCG's benchmarking study at https://www.113.vovici.net/se/13B2588B4D5FD030.

A people-centered approach to leading perpetual transformation

TONY O'DRISCOLL

13

Business is tough, and getting tougher. Since the year 2000, just over half of the names of companies on the Fortune 500 list have disappeared.[58] Today, the average life-span of a typical publicly traded company is two-and-a-half times shorter than the average life-span of a typical employee. Organizations are dying prematurely because they simply can't keep up with the intensifying levels of change and complexity within their business ecosystem.[59]

Ensuring organizational survival in the face of increased uncertainty presents a pernicious paradox for leaders. On one hand, they must continue to run their core business as efficiently as possible. On the other, they must develop and implement strategies to effectively change their business in response to swift and sweeping ecosystem shifts.[60]

To make matters worse, most transformation interventions focused on changing structure, governance and process are falling-flat.[61] Research reveals that organization transformation efforts fail more than 70 percent of the time.[62] In an ever-evolving business ecosystem where changing the business on an ongoing basis becomes table stakes for survival, the low level of transformation success and the increasing rate of organization mortality signal an urgent need for a fundamentally different, people-centered, approach to leading organizational change.

The People Centered Transformation (PCT) Framework

Brightline's People Manifesto argues that people form the link between strategy design and delivery.[63] People turn ideas into reality, they are the strategy in motion. People are the organization's most important source of competitive advantage and yet, paradoxically, they are often also the organization's most misunderstood and least leveraged asset.

Organizations cannot change unless their people change. Most transformation efforts fail because leadership overemphasizes the tangible side of change and under emphasizes the emotional one. Organization change works when you identify the key beliefs and behaviors you want to change and then create new structures, processes and governance mechanisms to support those new beliefs and behaviors.[64] Not the other way around.

Successful organization transformation requires an empathic, people-centered approach to change that nurtures a culture of aspiration, alignment, autonomy and accountability.[65] The remainder of this paper will explore the ten key elements of such a people-centered transformation (PCT) framework (see Figure 1).

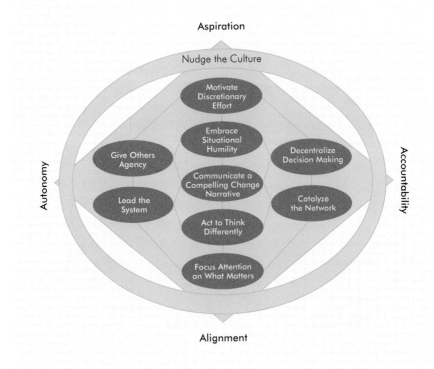

Figure 1: The People-Centered Transformation (PCT) Framework

Each element of the PCT framework requires three key leadership shifts to activate it. Successfully completing all the shifts across each of the ten elements, will yield an organization that is resilient, responsive and agile; a culture of aspiration, alignment, autonomy and accountability; and an employee base that is fully engaged and willing to tap into their discretionary effort and go the extra mile to make change really happen in your organization.

Next, we will examine the elemental insight, supporting evidence and leadership shifts for each PCT element in the framework.

PCT Element 1: Create a compelling change narrative

The Elemental Insight: On 18 August 1963, in his renowned speech on the steps of the Lincoln Memorial, Martin Luther King did not say 'I have a plan.' Instead, he shared a dream that led to the passing of the Civil Rights Act on 2 July 1964.

Since transformation efforts require a change in the status quo, communicating a compelling narrative that makes a purposeful, passionate and emotionally resonant case for the change motivates people to let go of the status quo and reach beyond their comfort zones to create a brighter shared future.

In essence, people need to believe that the achievement of a shared aspiration is possible and worthy of their effort before they are willing to change their behavior to make it happen. Creating and communicating a credible and compelling image of a desired future that people can create together motivates this behavioral change.

The Supporting Evidence: Leadership is the art of getting things done through other people. Daniel Goleman's research argues that leadership's primary task is to articulate a message that resonates with people's emotional reality and sense of purpose.[66] A research paper by Nathan Witta and Orla Leonard shows that teams who successfully deliver against transformational objectives spend 54 percent more time setting direction and crafting an aspiration that serves as a guiding light.[67]

The Leadership Shifts: In order to communicate a clear, concise, consistent and compelling narrative that makes a purposeful, passionate and emotionally resonant case for change, leadership behavior must **shift from**:

- focusing on required actions **to** creating a shared aspiration.
- stressing the problematic present **to** envisioning a positive future.
- monitoring the actionable what and how **to** illuminating the purposeful why.

PCT Element 2: Act to think differently

The Elemental Insight: With regards to leading change, Mahatma Gandhi embodied his belief that 'You must be the change you want to see in the world.'

In essence, authentic and visible changed behavior on the part of leadership is the single longest lever to motivate changed behavior within an organization. Leadership can generate respect and followership from others by personally, authentically and openly modeling the changed beliefs and behaviors needed to transform the organization.

The Supporting Evidence: While conventional wisdom holds that changing the way a person thinks can change the way they behave, recent research in the behavioral sciences suggest that the quickest path to changed behavior goes in the opposite direction: Getting someone to act differently can dramatically change their thinking.[68] Herminia Ibarra's research has shown that leaders who deliberately 'act their way into a new way of thinking' are more successful in changing their own behavior and in motivating changed behavior in others.[69]

The Leadership Shifts: In order to generate respect and followership from others by personally, authentically and openly modeling the changed beliefs and behaviors required to transform organizations, leadership behavior must shift from:

- demanding changed behavior **to** demonstrating changed behavior.
- being authoritarian and overbearing **to** being authentic and open.
- thinking and planning ahead of time **to** testing and learning in real time.

PCT Element 3: Embrace situational humility

The Elemental Insight: Almost a century ago, in 1924, the organizational pioneer Mary Parker Follett observed, 'Leadership is not defined by the exercise of power, but by the capacity to increase the sense of power among those led.'

In essence, the reality today is that individual leaders do not have the capacity, expertise or experience to make sense of all the change swirling around them. Instead, they need to distribute leadership responsibility, complementing hierarchy and formal authority with a collaborative and distributed leadership system that is responsive, resilient and adaptable to change.

The Supporting Evidence: To build a collaborative and distributed leadership system, leaders must embrace what Amy Edmondson calls 'situational humility' by showing vulnerability, seeking help, asking questions and demonstrating that failure is acceptable. Humility helps build a foundation of trust and psychological safety that gives others the confidence to engage in open, transparent and authentic interactions around change.[70] Research by Alison Reynolds and David Lewis has shown that the trusted reciprocal interaction derived from showing humility is crucial to ensuring that people can successfully work together to make change happen.[71]

The Leadership Shifts: In order to show vulnerability, seek help, demonstrate that failure is acceptable and constantly seek to increase the autonomy and accountability of others, leadership behavior must shift from:

- projecting power **to** showing vulnerability.
- demanding definitive answers **to** asking open questions.
- playing it safe **to** making failure safe.

PCT Element 4: Focus attention on what matters

The Elemental Insight: Upon his return to Apple as CEO in 1997, Steve Jobs eliminated more than 70 percent of Apple's products to bring strategic clarity and focus to his organization's efforts. In addressing Apple employees during this difficult transition, Jobs' message was simple: 'Focus is about saying no.'

In essence, most transformation efforts are undermined by an overload of projects and change initiatives and insufficient resources to make them happen. Also, as the number of organization change initiatives increase, so too does the potential for collaborative overload that can burn employees out and sap their motivation and productivity.

The Supporting Evidence: Yves Morieux's research shows that companies today set themselves six times as many performance requirements as they did in 1955. Back then, CEOs committed to between four and seven performance imperatives; today they commit to between 25 and 40.[72] Ron Carucci's research found that, in companies that successfully execute their strategies, 76 percent limit the number of initiatives they focus on.[73] Research from the Project Management Institute highlights that to reduce collaborative overload, leaders must adopt a portfolio-based approach to change by ensuring that people's attention and energy are squarely focused on the vital few change initiatives that matter most to the business.[74]

The Leadership Shifts: In order to focus attention on what matters most by prioritizing and communicating the key strategic priorities that matter most to the business, leadership behavior must shift from:
- monitoring project activity **to** focusing strategic attention.
- letting projects flow **to** pruning project portfolios.
- holding multiple options **to** enacting disciplined prioritization.

PCT Element 5: Motivate discretionary effort

The Elemental Insight: Legendary football coach Vince Lombardi, who led the Green Bay Packers to five NFL championships and two Super Bowls during the 1960s, said, 'Individual commitment to a group effort — that's what makes a team work, a company work, a society work.'

In essence, discretionary effort is what people choose to do above and beyond what is required of them by the organization. As such, it represents a significant source of potential energy to drive change. Unfortunately, the power of discretionary effort lies dormant in organizations today as the vast majority of employees are not engaged.

The Supporting Evidence: Gallup's research shows that only 35 percent of employees are highly involved in, enthusiastic about and committed to their work and workplace.[75] John P. Meyer and Marylène Gagné found that, to activate discretionary effort, leaders must focus on the intrinsic motivational levers that compel people to go the extra mile by tapping into their innermost aspirations and giving them autonomy in return for accountability.[76]

The Leadership Shifts: In order to motivate discretionary effort by tapping into the aspirations of others and giving them autonomy in return for accountability, leadership behavior must shift from:

- dictating direction **to** channelling aspiration.
- manipulating with fear **to** motivating with inspiration.
- requiring procedural conformity **to** recognizing novel effort.

PCT Element 6: Give others agency

The Elemental Insight: Charlene Li, an expert on digital transformation, defines agency as, 'The permission to take independent action or make changes without approval.'

In essence, organizations that give their people agency are far more likely to succeed in organization transformation efforts. That being said, agency must be a two-way street. The power to take independent action comes with the responsibility to make decisions and take actions, and it also carries the accountability for the outcome of those decisions and actions.

The Supporting Evidence: In giving others agency, Kevin Kruse's research shows that determining who leads and who follows is no longer defined by an individual's leadership position. Instead, leadership becomes a give-and-take process of social influence to maximize the efforts of others toward the achievement of their shared aspiration.[77]

The Leadership Shifts: In order to create agency by giving others permission to take independent actions and make changes without hierarchical approval, leadership behavior must shift from:

- exercising executive authority **to** giving individual agency.
- imposing top-down hierarchy **to** encouraging give-and-take reciprocity.
- requiring hierarchical permission **to** allowing independent action.

PCT Element 7: Decentralize decision making

The Elemental Insight: Roger Martin, former Dean of the Rotman School of Management at the University of Toronto, sees organizations as 'decision factories' and argues that leaders should only make the choices they are best equipped to make, clearly explain the rationale behind their choices, clarify the choices others should make and define the boundaries within which to make them.

In essence, organizations can maximize their effectiveness and efficiency by giving up centralized decision-making control and allowing decisions to be made where timeliness and expertise optimally intersect. Unfortunately, it appears that while the transformational benefits of giving up control around decision making are clear, leadership's willingness to decentralize decisions is lacking.

The Supporting Evidence: A Harvard Business School study found that 54 percent of organizations recognized as transformation leaders have decentralized decision making, compared with only 15 percent of transformation laggards.[78] Peter Drucker once observed, 'In most organizations, the bottlenecks is at the top of the bottle.' Research by Rob Cross and Laurence Prusak shows that leaders who are unwilling to let go of decision-making control slow the organization down.[79]

The Leadership Shifts: In order to make only the choices they are best equipped to make, clarify the choices others have to make and the boundaries within which to make them, leadership behavior must shift from:

- centralizing decisions **to** distributing decision making.
- deciding based on position/role **to** deciding based on expertise/experience.
- expecting agreement on decisions **to** explaining rationale for decisions.

PCT Element 8: Catalyze the network

The Elemental Insight: John Kotter of Harvard Business School argues that organizations seeking to transform must create a 'second operating system' devoted to the dynamic design and delivery of strategy using an agile, network-like structure.

In essence, running the business happens vertically while changing it happens horizontally. The traditional hierarchical structures, optimized for the efficient vertical command-and-control of operations, is not fit for purpose to effectively navigate horizontal, cross-functional change. Creating a second operating system to change the business requires that leaders exercise their position power and influence to override the traditional hierarchy, creating time and space for teams to emerge, converge and engage around critical cross-functional interfaces.

The Supporting Evidence: An EIU/Brightline study found that organizations that excel at changing their business purposefully orchestrate dynamic connections and interactions between those who design a change initiative and those who deliver it.[80] To enable these interactions, a *Harvard Business Review* research report found that leaders must make silos irrelevant, place a premium on organization agility and nurture an ecosystem of self-organizing cross-functional teams.[81]

The Leadership Shifts: In order for leaders to create the time and space for cross-functional teams to emerge, converge and engage around critical strategy-design interfaces, their behavior must shift from:

- leveraging organization hierarchies **to** activating informal networks.
- restructuring organizational charts **to** reconfiguring organizational networks.
- assigning cross-functional teams **to** enabling emergent collaborative teaming.

PCT Element 9: Lead the system

The Elemental Insight: Systems thinker Peter Senge maintains that 'real change starts with recognizing that we are part of the systems we seek to change,' and argues that we need a new kind of leader — a systems leader — to catalyze the collaborative leadership required to successfully navigate dynamic, complex and systemic change.

In essence, in adaptive-leadership systems, the role of leadership is not to control but to catalyze. Catalyzing an adaptive-leadership system requires a fundamental paradigm shift from leaders about what it means to lead. Leaders must recognize that their catalytic role is not to exercise vertical control but to encourage horizontal collaboration. It is not about enforcing rules, it is about nurturing relationships. It is not about exerting power over others but generating energy within and among others. It is not about mandating individual responsibility but creating collective 'response-ability.'

The Supporting Evidence: Research by Kathleen Eisenhardt and Henning Piezunka reveals that a systems-based approach to leadership not only enhances the horizontal collaboration needed for value creation but also crates the conditions within which complex behavior emerges, resulting in the ability of the organization to coevolve with its environment.[82] Research from Deloitte shows that organizations that focus on developing systemic-level leadership capabilities attain 37 percent higher revenue per employee and nine percent higher gross profit margin, and are five times more likely to be highly effective at anticipating and responding to change.[83]

The Leadership Shifts: In order for leaders to catalyze the collaborative leadership required to successfully navigate dynamic, complex and systemic change, their behavior must shift from:

- exercising hierarchical leadership **to** activating systemic leadership.
- controlling and monitoring compliance **to** catalyzing and guiding change.
- applying technical leadership practices **to** enabling adaptive leadership systems.

PCT element 10: Nudge the culture

The Elemental Insight: Upon completing one of the largest and most successful transformations in business history, then IBM CEO Lou Gerstner said, 'I came to see in my time at IBM that culture isn't one aspect of the game, it is the game,' and went on to write a book titled *Who Says Elephants Can't Dance?*

Edgar Schein defines culture as 'The sum total of all the shared, taken-for-granted assumptions that a group has learned throughout its history.' He further asserts that culture cannot be separated from strategy because strategic thinking is deeply colored by these tacit assumptions. Culture, therefore, not only impedes the delivery of a strategy designed to change the business but also influences the design of the strategy in a limiting way. While culture itself is notoriously hard to change, it cannot be left to chance. The process of changing an organization is deeply rooted in nudging its culture towards aspiration, alignment, autonomy and accountability.

In essence, while an organization's survival depends on having the agility to respond and adapt to change, its culture acts as a limiting and resistive force to change. Organizational agility is no longer optional. Every organization, it appears, needs to learn the agility dance.

The Supporting Evidence: Bill Joiner, CEO of business consultancy CEO of ChangeWise, defines agility as 'the ability to take sustained effective action amid conditions of accelerating change and mounting complexity.' A recent PMI/Forbes Insights paper shows that 92 percent of respondents considered organizational agility to be crucial to business success,[84] while a McKinsey survey found that less than 25 percent of organizations consider themselves to be agile.[85]

The leadership shifts: In order for leaders to catalyze the collaborative leadership required to successfully navigate dynamic, complex and systemic change, their behavior must shift from:

- managing tangible aspects of change **to** addressing emotional side of change.
- tackling culture directly **to** activating the PCT elements.
- leaving culture change to chance to actively nudging the culture.

The PCT Call to Action

Martin Luther King did not have a plan. He had a dream that changed the course of history.

As a leader are you willing to change your own beliefs and behaviors to cultivate a culture that enables your organization to achieve its highest aspirations?

The four tenets of Brightline's People Manifesto are that followership matters as much as leadership, collaborative efforts must be strategically focused, culture can't be left to chance, and people must believe in the change.[86]

The People-Centered Transformation (PCT) Framework is purposefully designed to activate these tenets by:

1. Purposefully placing belief and behavior ahead of structure, process and governance
2. Prioritizing the PCT element requiring attention within your organization
3. Putting in place a plan to activate the leadership shifts within the priority PCT element

Martin Luther King also said, 'You don't have to see the whole staircase, just take the first step.' Take the first step in your People-Centered Transformation journey by completing the PCT pulse and identifying which of the PCT elements requires your immediate attention (see Figure 2).

From there, review the insights and research that describe your priority PCT element and develop a specific plan of action to model the three leadership shifts required to activate that PCT element. Repeat this process on a routine basis to constantly and continuously nudge your organization's culture towards aspiration, alignment, autonomy and agency, creating the agility required to sustain your enterprise in increasingly changeable and complex times.

Happy PCT Trails!

People-Centered Transformation Elements	Strongly Disagree	Neutral	Strongly Agree
1. Our leaders communicate a clear, concise, consistent and compelling narrative that makes a purposeful, passionate and emotionally resonant case for change	○ ○ ○	○ ○	○ ○ ○
2. Our leaders generate respect and followership from others by personally, authentically and openly modeling the changed beliefs and behaviors required to evolve the organization	○ ○ ○	○ ○	○ ○ ○
3. Our leaders show vulnerability, seek help, demonstrate that failure is acceptable, and consistently seek to increase the autonomy and accountability of others	○ ○ ○	○ ○	○ ○ ○
4. Our leaders bring clarity and focus by prioritizing and communicating the key strategic priorities that matter most to the business	○ ○ ○	○ ○	○ ○ ○
5. Our leaders understand how to motivate discretionary effort by tapping into the aspirations of others and giving them autonomy in return for accountability	○ ○ ○	○ ○	○ ○ ○
6. Our leaders create agency by giving others the permission to take independent actions and make changes without hierarchical approval	○ ○ ○	○ ○	○ ○ ○
7. Our leaders only make the choices they are best equipped to make, clarify the choices others have to make and the boundaries within which to make them	○ ○ ○	○ ○	○ ○ ○
8. Our leaders create the time and space for cross-functional teams to emerge, converge and engage around crucial strategy design and delivery interfaces	○ ○ ○	○ ○	○ ○ ○
9. Our leaders catalyze the collaborative leadership required to successfully navigate dynamic, complex and systemic change	○ ○ ○	○ ○	○ ○ ○
10. Our leaders consciously and continuously nudge the culture in the direction of aspiration, alignment, autonomy and accountability	○ ○ ○	○ ○	○ ○ ○

Figure 2: The People-Centered Transformation (PCT) Pulse

About the author

Tony O'Driscoll is an adjunct professor at Duke University's Fuqua School of Business and a Research Fellow at Duke Corporate Education. At Fuqua, he played a key role in redesigning Fuqua's Cross Continent MBA program and served as Executive Director of Fuqua's Center for Technology Entertainment and Media. During his 18-year corporate career, Tony was a founding member of IBM Global Service's Strategy and Change consulting practice and a member of IBM's Almaden Services Research group where he investigated the changing roles of leadership, innovation, and collaboration as enterprises become more global, virtual, open and digitally mediated. He launched and led Duke CE's Asia office, headquartered in Singapore.

Footnotes

58   Nanterme, P. (2016), 'Digital disruption has only just begun', World Economic Forum web article. https://www.weforum.org/agenda/2016/01/digital-disruption-has-only-just-begun/

59   Reeves, M. Levin, S. and Ueda. D. (2016), 'The biology of corporate survival', *Harvard Business Review*, January-February. https://hbr.org/2016/01/the-biology-of-corporate-survival

60   O'Driscoll, Tony (2019), 'Catalyze an adaptive leadership system', *Dialogue* online. http://dialoguereview.com/catalyse-an-adaptive-leadership-system/

61   Reynolds, A. and Lewis, D. (2017), 'Closing the strategy-execution gap means focusing on what employees think, not what they do', *Harvard Business Review* online. https://hbr.org/2017/10/closing-the-strategy-execution-gap-means-focusing-on-what-employees-think-not-what-they-do

62   Speculand, R. (2017), *Excellence in Execution: How to Implement Your Strategy* (New York: Morgan James).

63   Brightline (2019), *People Manifesto*. https://www.brightline.org/people-manifesto/

64   Li, Charlene. (2019), *The Disruption Mindset* (Ideapress Publishing).

65   Brightline Initiative/HBS Research Report (2019), *Testing Organizational Boundaries to Improve Strategy Execution*. https://www.brightline.org/resources/testing-organizational-boundaries-to-improve-strategy-execution/

66   Goleman, D. (1995), Emotional Intelligence: *Why It Can Matter More Than IQ* (London: Bantam Books).

67   Wiita, N. and Leonard, O. (2017), 'How the most successful teams bridge the strategy-execution gap', Harvard Business Review. https://hbr.org/2017/11/how-the-most-successful-teams-bridge-the-strategy-execution-gap

68   Zenger, J. (2019), 'A surefire way to improve your leadership (but only a few will do it)', Forbes. www.forbes.com/sitesjackzenger/2019/11/15/a-surefire-way-to-improve-your-leadership-but-only-a-few-will-do-it/#46540b7e68f0

69   Ibarra, H. (2015), *Act Like a Leader, Think Like a Leader* (HBR Press). https://knowledge. insead.edu/blog/insead-blog/how-to-act-and-think-like-a-leader-3894

70   Brightline Initiative (2019), *Testing Organizational Boundaries to Improve Strategy Execution*, Harvard Business Review, April. www.brightline.org/resources/testing-organizational-boundaries-to-improve-strategy-execution/

71   Reynolds, A. and Lewis, D. (2017), 'Closing the strategy-execution gap means focusing on what employees think, not what they do', Harvard Business Review. https://hbr.org/2017/10/closing-the-strategy-execution-gap-means-focusing-on-what-employees-think-not-what-they-do

72   Morieux, Y. (2011), 'Smart rules, six ways to get people to solve problems without you', Harvard Business Review. https://hbr.org/2011/09/smart-rules-six-ways-to-get-people-to-solve-problems-without-you

73   Carucci, R. (2017), 'Executives fail to execute strategy because they're too internally focused', Harvard Business Review. https://hbr.org/2017/11/executives-fail-to-execute-strategy-because-theyre-too-internally-focused

74   PMI/EIU (2013), *Why Good Strategies Fail*. www.pmi.org/-/media/pmi/documents/public/pdf/learning/thought-leadership/why-good-strategies-fail-report.pdf

75   Gallup (2021), 'U.S employee engagement rises following wild 2020'. www.gallup.com/workplace/330017/employee-engagement-rises-following-wild-2020.aspx

76   Meyer, J. P. and Gangé, M. (2008), 'Employee engagement from a self determination theory perspective', Industrial and Organization Psychology 1(1): 60–62. https://selfdeterminationtheory.org/SDT/documents/2008_MeyerGagne_IOP.pdf.

77   Kruse, K. (2013), 'What is leadership?' Forbes. www.forbes.com/sites/kevinkruse/2013/04/09/what-is-leadership/#781856765b90

78   *Harvard Business Review* (2019).

79   Cross, R. and Prusak, L. (2002). The People Who Make Organizations Go-or Stop. Harvard Business Review: https://hbr.org/2002/06/the-people-who-make-organizations-go-or-stop

80   Brightline Initiative/EIU (2017). Closing the Gap: Designing and Delivering a Strategy that Works: www.brightline.org/resources/eiu-report/

81   *Harvard Business Review* (2019).

82   Eisenhardt, K. M. and Piezunka, H. (2011), 'Complexity Theory and corporate strategy', in The SAGE Handbook of Complexity and Management (London: Sage), pp. 56–9.

83   Brightline Initiative/EIU (2017).

84   PMI, F.I. (2017), *Achieving Greater Agility: The Essential Influence of the C-Suite*. www.pmi.org/learning/thought-leadership/series/achieving-greater-agility/essential-influence-c-suite

85   McKinsey (2017), *How to Create an Agile Organization*. www.mckinsey.com/business-functions/organization/our-insights/how-to-create-an-agile-organization

86   Brightline (2018), *The People Manifesto*. https://www.brightline.org/people-manifesto/

Transformation ignition points

TAHIROU ASSANE, YAVNIKA KHANNA,
EMIL ANDERSSON AND TONY O'DRISCOLL

14

Making sense of transformation — and the idea of perpetual transformation — is undoubtedly a demanding task. But, while each situation in an organization feels very different, the reality is that there are shared experiences, fears and hopes around all transformations. There are foundational issues which need to be tackled. There are many lessons which can be learned from the experiences of others.

In its work, Brightline, a Project Management Institute Initiative, has researched and canvassed the views and experiences of thousands of executives throughout the world. It has also engaged directly with the world's leading thinkers on transformation. The same — frequently challenging — questions occur time and time again. This article brings together the questions we have heard most. This is not to suggest that the answers to the questions are straightforward, but by knowing the most likely questions and to have given them some thought, transformation leaders begin the process of preparation.

Ignition Point #1: Are your eyes and ears open?

Sangeet Paul Choudary, coauthor of *The Platform Revolution*, maps out the new reality: "Technological shifts continue to accelerate, and artificial intelligence is rapidly advancing across sectors. More importantly, traditional industry boundaries are disappearing, often leading to creation of new value pools and business models where none existed in the past. Geopolitically, the rise of China is reshaping the global economic order and the rise of stakeholder capitalism will further create new value pools as business priorities shift to embrace larger societal and environmental value. Finally, investor activism and regulatory shifts will also play an important role in determining future value pools."[87] He argues that the ability of executives to benefit from such shifts is dependent on three factors: how early they spot the shift, their ability to innovate and reconfigure their business model portfolio to position themselves in the new value pool, and the strength of the control point that consolidates their position in this new value pool.

Awareness is everything. "There are myriad reasons why successful companies are unable to adapt their enterprises to transformational market shifts and cascade into rapid decline," writes Jeff Kuhn in his contribution to this collection. He goes on to identify these barriers to transformation as:

- Structural and cultural inertia
- Fear of cannibalizing the core business
- Stick to your knitting syndrome
- The curse of success
- Missing or dismissing the weak signals of change
- Frozen mental models
- Short-termism and incrementalism
- Lack of foresight and imagination.

The starting question in any would-be transformation must be whether the management team is alive to these potential blockers to change of any sort. As Zhang Ruimin CEO of the Chinese white goods company Haier puts it: "There is no such thing as a successful company. There are only companies that move with the times."

And the very human temptation is to refuse to do so. A March 2020 *Sloan Management Review* article by Scott Anthony and Michael Putz argues that the fundamental problem is that organizations are run by... humans, that suffer from biases and blind spots that lead them to systematically underestimate the threat of and overestimate the difficulty of responding to disruptive change.[88] A thirst for perpetual transformation effectively works against human nature and its appetite for the status quo.

Ignition Point #2: What is a transformation?

It is then useful to begin, as always, by defining terms. What do you actually mean by a transformation? Many different companies, scholars, and experts have defined what it means to them. According to the Project Management Institute, "transformation refers to an organization achieving a sustainable quantum-leap improvement in performance while transforming the mindsets of employees and thus the culture of the organization."[89]

These other descriptions of transformation are great places to start in your discussions:

"A comprehensive change in strategy, operating model, organization, people, and processes to achieve a dramatic improvement in performance and alter a company's future trajectory."

Lars Fæste, Jim Hemerling, Perry Keenan, and Martin Reeves.[90]

"There are three processes that approach change in critically different ways. Improving operations to drive efficiency by reducing costs, improving quality and service and reducing development time. Strategic transformation seeks to redefine business objectives, create new competencies and harness these capabilities to meet market opportunities. Corporate self-renewal creates the ability for a firm to anticipate and cope with change so that strategic and operational gaps do not develop."
Barbara Blumenthal and Philippe Haspelagh.[91]

"Transformation comes in three different forms: operational, core and strategic. Operational focuses on doing what you're currently doing better, faster or cheaper using new technologies to solve old problems. Core focuses on doing what you are currently doing in a fundamentally different way. Strategic focuses on changing the very essence of your company.
Scott Anthony.[92]

"Transformation is a significant, lasting and nonreversible change to the company's value creation logic."
Haig Barrett and Christian Rangen.[93]

"Transformation is foremost a continuing process. It does not have an end point. Transformation is meant to create or anticipate the future. Transformation is meant to deal with the coevolution of concepts, processes, organizations and technology. Change in any one of these areas necessitates change in all. Transformation is meant to create new competitive areas and new competencies. Transformation is meant to identify, leverage and even create new underlying principles for the way things are done. Transformation is meant to identify and leverage new sources of power."
Ronald O'Rourke.[94]

Ignition Point #3: What is the context in which your transformation is taking place?

Of course, in any organization here are many things to consider when initiating a transformation: "Do we need to reorganize the company? Should we look into partnerships or acquisitions? What about digitization? What processes can be automated at our company?" Questions like these are hard to answer at first because they're missing the bigger picture: the context in which your transformation is taking place. Once you can adequately describe a transformation, it's important to clarify that all transformations typically begin at the strategic level.

What can you do to properly analyze this context? Begin by considering two important factors: the *degree of complexity* and the *rate of change*. These are external and exogenous variables. The business does not necessarily have control of them. Rather they set the operating context within which the business must work to deliver value.

You can consider the degree of your organization's complexity in four stages:
Simple: We know exactly where we are going, and we know exactly how to get there

Complicated: We have a good idea where we want to go and there are a number of pathways that could get us there

Complex: There are a range of possible directions we could go in and the pathways to get there are different

Chaos: We do not know where we are going, and we have no idea how to get there.

Similarly, you can consider the rate of change in your organization in four stages:
Constant: Our operating environment is constant

Velocity: Our operating environment is moving at steady velocity

Acceleration: Our operating environment is accelerating faster and faster

Jerk: Our operating environment is accelerating so much we are reaching a breaking point. Jerk is the term in physics for acceleration over time.

When you establish the rate of change *and* the degree of complexity, you can then determine your level of uncertainty. The relationship is not linear, but exponential: the higher the degree of complexity and rate of change, the more uncertain things become.

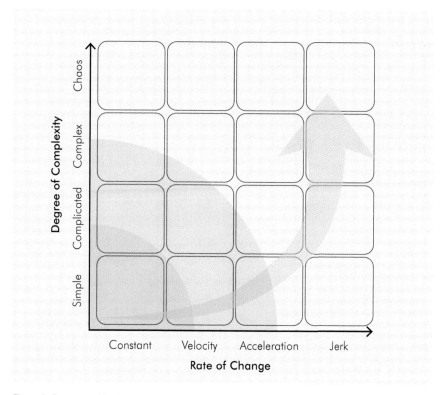

Figure 1: Determining Your Uncertainty Zone

Ignition Point #4: Are you being disrupted at the level of your operating model, infrastructure model or business model?

In *Zone to Win*, Geoffrey Moore identifies the Waves of Change which articulate the appropriate strategic posture that the business should employ, based on where they are situated in the levels of uncertainty.[95]

- **Wave 1: Infrastructure Model Change.** This wave defines an organization that needs to improve operations, distribution, and support to make the organization more efficient.
- **Wave 2: Operating Model Change.** This wave defines an organization that needs to develop new products and services, explore new geographic markets and distribution channels, and create new support and production approaches and technologies.
- **Wave 3: Business Model Change.** This wave is a radical change of the business model to position the organization for long term growth, offering protection from disruption.

The key is that real transformation lies beyond Wave 1. By only focusing on Wave 1, we are increasing the efficiency of the Titanic by optimizing the structure, processes and routines in the engine room in order to speed up the ship. However, this overly inward focus on efficiency and speed could miss the disruptive iceberg lurking on the horizon. Wave 1 embraces many digital transformations.

Ignition Point #5: What's the time horizon?

The horizon framework introduces time and gets more specific about what the strategy response should be from a competitive perspective. It is more granular and prescriptive. Companies need to focus equally on all three business horizons to make sure they don't get stuck by focusing only on their current products, services and markets. By focusing on all three, you can analyze opportunities for growth, while maintaining your core business functions.

In **Horizon 1** the goal is to outcompete your existing competitors using efficiency while also mining your existing core business to the max. The immediacy of this can easily overwhelm other efforts important to the future of a company.

The goal in **Horizon 2** is to out-innovate your competitors by both extending your core in new and novel ways but also in identifying new customer needs that require the business to move to a new core.

The goal in **Horizon 3** is to reshape the business landscape by collaborating with complementary organizations in new growth arenas defined by emerging customer needs. In this horizon, the organization simultaneously changes to a new core business while partnering with other organizations with complementary capabilities to collaboratively fulfill customer needs.

Companies must manage businesses along all three horizons concurrently. C-suite leaders can use this horizon model as a blueprint for balancing attention in current performance and opportunities for growth.

Ignition Point #6: What IS the transformation that you will be initiating?

So how can we take these strategic concepts and apply them to our work? Consider two concrete ideas: **What We Do** — this can also be expressed as the source of value differentiation, and it can fall anywhere between existing and new — and **How We Do It** — this is the means of value delivery and can also fall anywhere between existing and new.

Within this more initiative-oriented mindset, three domains of transformation can be identified:

- **Productive Transformation** makes today's business better, cheaper and faster.
- **Core Transformation** provides value in different ways to different customers.
- **Strategic Transformation** changes the essence and value creation logic of your company.

Another way of describing this is in the words of Chris Zook of Bain is that at one end of the spectrum, the business is exploiting the core while on the other, the business is exploring the edge.[96] Exploiting the core means maximizing core business profitability by applying the best practices and technology to drive efficiency and productivity. Exploring the edge is where the business will aim to uncover and maximize new growth opportunities by creative means. Both require ambidextrous focus, mindsets, and ways of working. This is, of course, easier said than done.

Ignition Point #7: Does your organization have the requisite capabilities to achieve its transformation objective?

Brightline's research reveals that overcoming the capability gap is the greatest challenge in transformations. Few organizations will have all the experience, attributes and resources that are required to deliver the enterprise-level change they desire. The talent guru Dave Ulrich defines a business capability as "a particular ability or capacity that a business may possess or exchange to achieve a specific purpose or outcome. A capability describes what the business does that creates value for customers."[97]

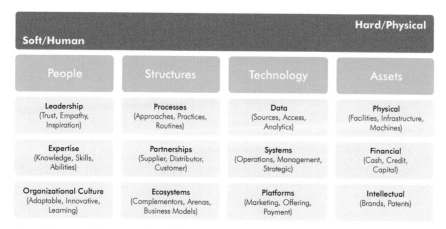

Figure 2: Assessing Transformation Capabilities

Any assessment of an organization's capabilities must begin with **people capabilities**. Peter Drucker famously quipped that "Culture eats strategy" for breakfast. Most strategies fail, not because they are poorly formulated, but because they are poorly implemented. Researchers, Allison Reynolds, and David Lewis suggest that most transformation efforts fail due to what they describe as "the tyranny of the tangible," where organizations overemphasize the tangible aspects of transformation such as structure, technology, process and governance while largely ignoring the intangible areas such as employee competence and mindset. When it comes to successful transformation the soft stuff truly is the hard stuff.

People capabilities cover three areas:
- **Leadership** — transformation leaders need to be dynamic and inspirational with a clear and shared vision. They must also be effective communicators, yet empathetic and willing to accept feedback.
- **Expertise** — employees around the organization need to have adequate tacit knowledge in their functional areas to support the transformation effort.
- **Organizational Culture** — the culture needs to reflect a collaborative, safe and nurturing work environment.

It is easy to say how important people are, but it is often difficult to translate the recognition of this importance into implementation. There are subtle skills which need careful development, individually and organizationally. Our own research at Brightline suggests that hiring and retaining top-notch talent facilitates a smoother journey for transformation.[98] But, make no mistake, ensuring you have the right people in the right places with the right skills is a big challenge.

In fact, the two top success factors for implementing strategic transformation include possession of "sufficient resources" and "existing talent with the right skillset."[99] In terms of people capabilities, it is worth asking: What skill improvements do we need (soft and hard)? Who are the transformation leaders and champions in our organization? How can we best support them? Are we hiring the best people with a diversity of ideas? And, in terms of culture change, what should your people think and feel about the organization?

While people capabilities are the most vitally important, clearly any transformation demands other organizational capabilities managed in symbiosis:

Structural capabilities

Processes — processes need to be efficient, while also being flexible enough to change without hindering progress.

Partnerships — partnerships with other organizations need to be strong and collaborative.

Ecosystems — the organization needs to be wholly aware of the ecosystem in which it operates, including competitors, consumer demand and any potential market disruptors.

Research shows that high-performing organizations tend to be more adaptable to change while also effectively employing formalized and standardized frameworks and processes.[100] The fact that effective frameworks and processes designed to foster flexibility and autonomy lead to faster transformation leaves us with several questions: Do the current frameworks in place empower the people and simplify the delivery processes? Are we reviewing lessons learned from past failures? Do we have strong partnerships fostering collaborative engagements? Are we fully aware of our ecosystem and the megatrends impacting it? Are we learning from competitors and peers in the ecosystem? Are we speaking with our customers and end users?

Technology capabilities

Data — information needs to be clean, organized and consist of only things that need to be assessed and/or utilized.

Systems — technology systems need to be intuitive and, ideally, as simple as possible.

Platforms — platforms need to be intuitive and made available for employees and customers to use effectively.

Technology is a hugely important factor and an enabler to value creation transformation in current times. It is worth considering some basic questions in thinking through your tech capabilities: What's your position on research and innovation? Do you need to be ahead or equal to the competition in research? Where are you innovating? Where do you need to be innovating? What is our ration of in-house technology expertise vs. contractors, third parties, or partners?

Assets

Physical Assets — office space, machinery, equipment, inventory and other such physical assets need to be organized and used efficiently (rather than being wasteful).

Financial Assets — assets need to be sufficiently allocated to prioritized activities, and budgets need to be frequently adjusted to reflect any costs and revenue over time.

Intellectual Assets — brand and patents are long-term assets taking time to build and must be treated with care.

To effectively organize and manage physical, financial and intellectual assets, an organization must continuously reassess and reprioritize allocation for each. Ask yourself: do we have the right assets in place for the transformation? Are the assets efficiently allocated? Do we continuously reassess and reprioritize assets based on needs, and can we quickly reallocate assets accordingly?

The next challenge is to identify the specific actions to take in order to close the capability gaps to ensure your organization is transformation ready. The ignition points are likely to lead to as many more questions and challenges as neat and tidy answers. There is no disguising the fact that transformation is hugely difficult. A recent survey of directors, CEOs and senior executives by the *Wall Street Journal* found that transformation risk is their number one concern. Little wonder. The *Harvard Business Review* reports that 70 percent of large-scale transformations fail to meet their goals

Forbes reports that $900 billion was wasted in digital transformation efforts in a single year. Such dismal statistics are not set in stone. They, like your organization, can and must be transformed. Start by paying attention to the seven ignition points.

About the authors

Tahirou Assane, MASc, P.Eng, PMP is Director of Brightline Project Management Institute.

Yavnika Khanna, MBA, PMP is Head of Partnerships of Brightline Project Management Institute.

Emil Andersson, MSc, is Project Manager in Research and Capability Building of Brightline Project Management Institute.

Tony O'Driscoll, is an adjunct professor at Duke University's Fuqua School of Business and Research Fellow at Duke Corporate Education.

Footnotes

87   Brightline/Thinkers50, *Transforming Beyond the Crisis*, Thinkers50 2020. https://www. brightline.org/resources/transforming-beyond-the-crisis/

88   Scott D. Anthony and Michael Putz, "How Leaders Delude Themselves About Disruption," *Sloan Management Review*, Spring 2020. https://sloanreview.mit.edu/article/how-leaders-delude-themselves-about-disruption/

89   Project Management Institute, The Brightline Transformation Compass: A Comprehensive System for Transformation, 2019. https://www.brightline.org/resources/transformation-compass/

90   Lars Fæste, Jim Hemerling, Perry Keenan and Martin Reeves, *Transformation: The Imperative to Change*. BCG Global, 3 November 2014. https://www.bcg.com/publications/2014/people-organization-transformation-imperative-change

91   Barbara Blumenthal and Philippe Haspelagh, "Toward a Definition of Corporate Transformation", *MIT Sloan Management Review*, 15 April 1994; https://sloanreview.mit.edu/article/toward-a-definition-of-corporate-transformation/

92   Scott Anthony, "What Do You Really Mean by Business 'Transformation'?" *Harvard Business Review*, 30 June 2016. https://hbr.org/2016/02/what-do-you-really-mean-by-business-transformation

93   Haig Barrett and Christian Rangen, "Closing the Transformation Gap: What steps can you take to bring about significant, lasting value for your organisation?" THE NEXT 20, 21 January 2019. https://haigbarrett.co.uk/2021/01/18/closing-the-transformation-gap-what-steps-can-you-take-to-bring-about-significant-lasting-value-for-your-organisation/

94   Ronald O'Rourke, *Defense Transformation: Background and Oversight Issues for Congress*, *CRS Report for Congress*. US Department of Defense, 9 November 2006; . https://fas.org/sgp/crs/natsec/RL32238.pdf

95   Geoffrey Moore, *Zone to Win: Organizing to Compete in an Age of Disruption*. Diversion Books, November 3. 2015.

96   https://www.bain.com/our-team/chris-zook/

97   Dave Ulrich, "Business Capability Map Definitions: What is a business capabilities model", Capstera, 7 February 2018. https://www.capstera.com/business-capability-map-definitions/

98   Strategic Transformation: Mastering Strategy Implementation in Transformative Times. Brightline Initiative of Project Management Institute. April 6, 2020. https://www.brightline.org/resources/strategic-transformation-research/

99   Strategic Transformation: Mastering Strategy Implementation in Transformative Times. Brightline Initiative of Project Management Institute. April 6, 2020. https://www.brightline.org/resources/strategic-transformation-research/

100 Strategic Transformation: Mastering Strategy Implementation in Transformative Times. Brightline Initiative of Project Management Institute. April 6, 2020. https://www.brightline.org/resources/strategic-transformation-research/

Transform for resilience: An imperative for good times too

MARTIN REEVES, LARS FÆSTE,
AND TOM DEEGAN

15

Durng the Covid-19 crisis, resilience rose to the top of the strategic agenda with many leaders also indicating a desire to extract lessons to increase preparedness for future crises. Although less emphasized in stable periods, our research indicates that resilience creates significant value and does so well beyond times of crisis. Nearly two-thirds of long-run outperformers do better than peers in response to shocks.

Crises often precipitate or accentuate the need to transform because of the immediate pressure on performance. Crisis-driven transformations often aim to ameliorate performance pressure by increasing cost and asset efficiency. But what is their impact on resilience and long-term performance? And how can companies transform for not only efficiency but also resilience?

To better understand the impact of large-scale change programs on building resilience, we applied an evidence-based approach to study 1,200+ corporate transformations over the last 25 years. The evidence indicates that roughly half of corporate transformations fail to improve resilience in response to future crises. Analyzing the same dataset also offers valuable insights into how some companies successfully transform for resilience.

Measuring the impact of a resilient transformation

To study the success factors of a resilient transformation, we must first quantify the total value created by resilient companies in response to crises. Our past research has identified three stages during which resilience creates value relative to peers:

- First, the immediate impact of a shock can be lower than peers by better absorbing the shock
- Second, they can have higher recovery speeds by rapidly adapting to new circumstances
- Finally, they can have a greater recovery extent (12-month period following a shock) by reimagining their business to flourish in new circumstances.

Cumulatively, the relative performance (TSR benchmarked to industry median) across all three stages is the total value of resilience displayed in response to a crisis.

Exhibit 1 | Total value of resilience realized across three stages

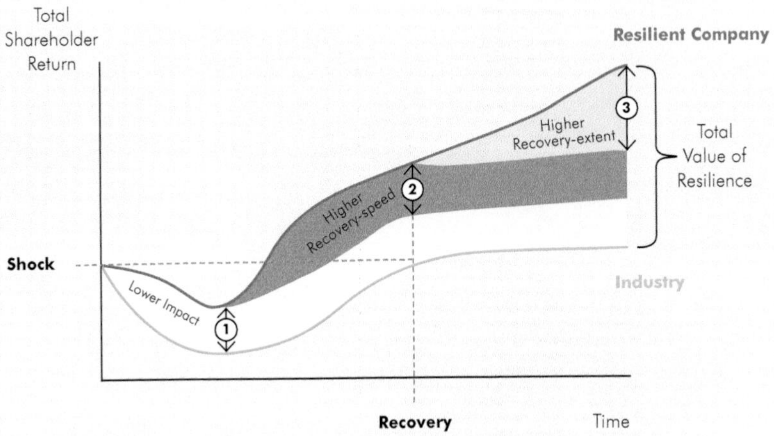

Source: BCG Henderson Institute Analysis

To measure the impact of change programs on resilience, we have studied the difference in total resilience in response to industry shocks during the 5-year period following a corporate transformation. While roughly half of transformations fail to improve resilience, a significant spread in outcomes exists. The top quartile of resilient transformations improved performance relative to industry by 25pp in response to future crises while the bottom quartile saw a decline of 20pp.

What can we learn from the outperformers?

1. **Growth acceleration is the main driver of a resilient transformation.** Whereas large-scale change programs, especially crisis-induced ones, typically target cost reduction, differential growth contributes most of the incremental value created by resilient transformations. Transformations that accelerate growth improve performance relative to industry during each stage of future crises (+6pp total impact on average) while transformations that only reduce costs see future resilience decline.

2. **Transformations that reduce debt and increase flexibility improve resilience.** Transformations that reduce debt loads improve the ability to cushion the immediate impact of a future shock.

Furthermore, transformations that reduce fixed asset intensity boost adaptivity and recovery speed by shifting costs toward variable expenses. Growth transformations that do both increase the odds of improving resilience from half to nearly two-thirds and yield an average change in TSR performance relative to industry of +10pp in response to future crises.

3. **Transformations are empirically less likely to build resilience when a crisis is no longer fresh.** If history is any guide, resilience now risks losing its spot on the corporate agenda as the performance of economies and companies recover. Immediately following a crisis, transformations are 19 percent more likely to be growth-oriented and 20 percent less likely to increase debt than those at least 12 months removed. However, our research shows that allowing resilience to fall off the change agenda would be a mistake. In today's dynamic business environment, resilience has benefits across the whole economic cycle.

Growth drives resilient transformations

Our past research indicates that transformations often aim primarily at reducing costs. While this may improve performance in the short run, on average, it does not lead to greater resilience in future crises. In contrast, transformations that accelerate growth, in aggregate, improve total resilience by +6pp while those that decelerate growth, on average, fail to improve resilience.

Exhibit 2 | Growth drives resilient transformations

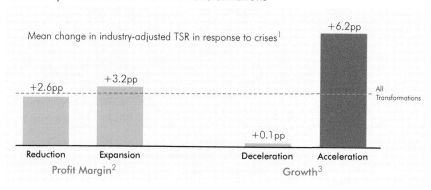

Mean change in industry-adjusted TSR in response to crises[1]

+6.2pp

+3.2pp

+2.6pp

All Transformations

+0.1pp

Reduction	Expansion		Deceleration	Acceleration
Profit Margin[2]			Growth[3]	

1. Crisis quarter if peak decline in industry TSR exceeds 15pp. Compares performance in response to industry shocks during 5-year periods preceding and following corporate transformation
2. Margin expansion if 12-month EBIT margin after transformation end is greater than 12-month EBIT margin before transformation start; reduction otherwise
3. Growth acceleration if trailing 12-month growth in full-year following end of transformation is greater than trailing 12-month growth at start of transformation; deceleration otherwise

Source: S&P Capital IQ; BCG Henderson Institute analysis

While growth transformations succeed in improving performance relative to industry during each of the three stages of future crises, nearly half of the improvement manifests in the extent of future recovery. In this third stage, after the recovery has taken hold, companies begin to reimagine their products and business models to thrive in the altered circumstances resulting from the shock. Growth-oriented transformations create significant advantage in this period by building the capability to spot and capitalize on new growth opportunities.

Exhibit 3 | Growth transformations especially advantage future recovery extent

Mean change in industry-adjusted TSR in response to crises[1]

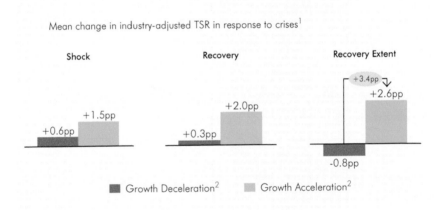

1. Crisis quarter if peak decline in industry TSR exceeds 15pp. Compares performance in response to industry shocks during 5-year periods preceding and following corporate transformation
2. Growth acceleration if trailing 12-month growth in full-year following end of transformation is greater than trailing 12-month growth at start of transformation; deceleration otherwise

Source: S&P Capital IQ; BCG Henderson Institute analysis

For example, NVIDIA's 2015 corporate transformation restructured operations toward strategic growth areas in deep learning, automated driving and gaming. Following the transformation, NVIDIA doubled its growth rate over the next 12 months to 26 percent. With the semiconductor industry recovering to prepandemic highs in June, NVIDIA once again shifted its strategic focus to identifying new growth drivers. In June 2020, the organization announced a partnership with Daimler AG unit Mercedes-Benz to build software-defined computing architecture for automated driving and in April 2021, unveiled the company's first data center GPU. Having previously performed in line with peers during post-recovery periods, NVIDIA has thus far outperformed industry peers by +11pp throughout the Covid-19 recovery.

Debt reduction and operational flexibility also help transformations that reduce debt loads help companies cushion future shocks. Large-scale change efforts often require a significant financial commitment. In response, leaders may find it tempting — particularly in the low interest rate environment of the last decade — to fund change programs by increasing corporate debt. But doing so materially reduces resilience on average.

When a crisis hits, highly leveraged companies are more likely to struggle to sustain operations as servicing debt is a higher fixed cost. It also limits the ability of corporations to tap into corporate debt markets during a future crisis — either to sustain operations or acquire distressed assets. Furthermore, investors often prefer the safety of corporations with lower debt levels amid the uncertainty of a crisis, compounding the problem.

Our research finds that growth transformations that reduce debt burdens (lower debt-to-enterprise value) increase performance relative to industry during future market dips by +2.5pp on average, while those that increase debt burdens see a decline of -0.3pp during the initial shock.

Consider The New York Times and its corporate transformation effort throughout the 2010s. After its debt burden briefly surpassed 200 percent of enterprise value during the global financial crisis, the company began rebalancing its portfolio of businesses and restructuring operations. After selling off several non-core business segments and entering a sale-leaseback agreement on its headquarters to free up capital, the organization began dramatically reducing debt and investing heavily in its paid digital subscription model. By the end of 2019, the organization announced it was debt free and had increased digital revenue to $800 million.

Without the higher burden of servicing debt, the organization was afforded a cushioning advantage as advertising revenue contracted sharply at the beginning of the Covid-19 crisis. Having struggled in past market shocks, The New York Times outperformed industry peers by +26pp during the first stage of the Covid-19 crisis.

Transformations that increase operational flexibility boost adaptivity. To succeed in crises — particularly during the recovery period, which can be unpredictable in timing and magnitude — companies need to rapidly adapt to the changing environment and scale up new models. Companies with greater operational flexibility (which we capture using the proxy of lower fixed asset intensity) can more easily adapt to outperform during the recovery stage.

Companies with lower levels of asset ownership tend to have a higher proportion of variable costs affording them the flexibility to tie costs closely to revenue in a downturn. They also tend to be less reliant on legacy assets, which creates an advantage in adapting to technological advances and seizing new market opportunities during the recovery. Our research shows that growth transformations that reduce fixed asset intensity increase performance relative to industry during future market recoveries by +3pp on average, while those that increase levels of fixed asset ownership see no change in performance during the recovery stage.

From 2004-06, consumer conglomerate Cendant Corporation undertook a strategic realignment to exit non-core business segments with high levels of fixed assets. Over the two-year transformation, the organization initiated public offerings and spun-off segments in tax services, real estate services, and fleet leasing — reducing fixed asset intensity from 35 percent to 9 percent in the process.

Renaming the firm Avis Budget Group, the organization refocused its efforts on its core vehicle rental operations. With vehicles acquired under repurchase agreements (that allow for return of vehicles to manufacturer at set monthly depreciated value), the company now benefits from a highly variable cost structure. With the ability to quickly de-fleet during a downturn — and scale up during recovery — Avis was well-positioned when the global financial crisis hit. One year past the initial shock from the global financial crisis, Avis was +62pp above pre-shock levels while industry peers had yet to fully recover.

Taken together, transformations that accelerate growth, reduce debt loads, and increase operational flexibility improve performance relative to industry peers by +10pp in response to future crises.

Exhibit 4 | Debt reduction and operational flexibility further improve resilience

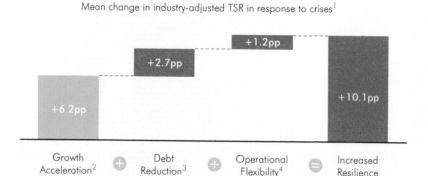

Mean change in industry-adjusted TSR in response to crises[1]

1. Crisis quarter if peak decline in industry TSR exceeds 15pp. Compares performance in response to industry shocks during 5-year periods preceding and following corporate transformation
2. Growth acceleration if trailing 12-month growth in full-year following end of transformation is greater than trailing 12-month growth at start of transformation; deceleration otherwise
3. Debt reduction defined as lower debt-EV ratio following transformation
4. Increased operational flexibility defined as lower fixed asset intensity (net PPE/sales) following transformation

Source: S&P Capital IQ; BCG Henderson Institute analysis

Don't overlook resilience in good times

The playbook for resilient transformations differs in a few ways from those which primarily aim to increase efficiency and optimize short-run financial performance. Transforming for resilience requires a new mindset which unfortunately tends to fade as stability and prosperity return.

When a crisis is fresh, our research indicates that leaders are more likely to adopt an approach to transformation that is consistent with building resilience. Immediately following a crisis, transformations are 19 percent more likely to be growth-oriented and 20 percent less likely to increase debt than those at least 12 months removed from a shock.

Put simply — as the crisis fades from memory leaders tend to neglect the importance of building resilience. Corporate change efforts tend to return to targeting cost reduction, stabilized corporate bond markets make debt financing more palatable, and the superior operational control afforded by asset ownership begins to look more attractive. Critically, however, the value of a resilient transformation remains the same — no matter the timing.

Future-oriented leaders recognize the long-term value of resilience and keep it on the change agenda in fair weather times. Based on our proprietary natural language processing analysis of SEC filings and annual reports, we find that transformations accompanied by a long-term strategic orientation are 10 percent more likely to accelerate growth, 30 percent more likely to reduce debt, and 24 percent more likely to reduced fixed asset ownership. For future-oriented leaders, keeping resilience on the transformation agenda pays off. Transformations that accelerate growth, reduce debt, and increase operational flexibility *in more stable periods* improve resilience by +7pp more than those that do not.

The resilient transformation agenda

The Covid-19 crisis has brought the value of corporate resilience into focus with many leaders now seeking to rebuild their organizations to be more resilient. While every transformation is unique, our findings point toward a pattern of moves that can improve the odds of a resilient transformation.

1. **Transform with an opportunity mindset.** Defensive, cost-cutting measures might produce short-term gains, but fail to advance resilience in the long-run. To build resilience — especially in the recovery stage of a crisis — corporate transformations must increase the organizational capacity for innovation and reinvention.
   Upstream of innovation lies imagination. Transformations that prioritize growth are those that increase the organizational ability to think counterfactually, break existing mental models, and conceive of the new ideas fitting for new environments. As such, transformations that push organizations to compete on imagination will be those best-positioned to thrive in altered circumstances after the next crisis.

2. **Accelerate digital transformation.** Digital transformations, executed correctly, can improve resilience by increasing operational flexibility and positioning the firm to capture new growth opportunities. Digital transformation can increase operational flexibility and adaptivity — both critical capabilities in improving recovery speeds in future. Some asset-light companies take this approach even further by organizing in massive digital ecosystems, effectively reducing asset intensity, pooling resources, spreading risk, and accelerating the scaling of new models and offerings.

Companies that build a digital technology advantage and strategically deploy it can further benefit by extending the perceptive power of the organization to identify emergent opportunities. Digital transformations can also free up human cognition to focus on higher-level activities, such as imagination, to conceive of new ideas and identify fresh sources of growth. In doing so, they create significant advantage in the final stage of future crises as organizations reinvent themselves to succeed in the new post-shock reality.

3. **Keep resilience on the transformation agenda in good times as well.** To capture the long-term competitive benefit of resilience in a very dynamic business environment, companies must transform with resilience in mind in stable times too.

Future crises are inevitable. Companies that recognize resilience as a long-term strategic imperative and make it a pillar of corporate change will be those best-positioned to outperform in future crises.

As corporations ready themselves for re-opening and growth, resilience is now at risk of losing the limelight. Change programs that prioritize growth over cost-cutting, debt reduction over debt financing, and operational flexibility over direct control, will realize the full value of resilience and build advantage for the next crisis.

About the authors

Martin Reeves is chairman of the BCG Henderson Institute. He is a managing director and senior partner in the Boston Consulting Group's San Francisco office. He is the co-author of *Your Strategy Needs a Strategy* (HBR Press, 2015) and *The Imagination Machine: How to Spark New Ideas and Create Your Company's Future* (HBR Press, 2021).

Lars Fæste is managing director and senior partner at the Boston Consulting Group's Hong Kong office.

Tom Deegan is a data scientist formerly at the BCG Henderson Institute.

The BCG Henderson Institute is Boston Consulting Group's strategy think tank, dedicated to exploring and developing valuable new insights from business, technology and science by embracing the powerful technology of ideas.

Perpetual transformation in a world in flux: Toward a flux mindset and organizational resilience

APRIL RINNE

16

A world in flux — and a future in flux — demands holistic rethinking of how business is done. From how we build, manage, grow and lead thriving companies, to expectations about talent and performance, to organizational culture: All of these things are up for reassessment and, potentially, a radical reshaping.

The global pandemic has been a wake-up call for a world in flux. Yet in many ways, they are but a warm-up for what lies ahead. I don't necessarily mean another pandemic (though now is no time to be complacent), but rather an era of constant, relentless and often seismic change. By and large, this world in flux does not align with how we've been taught to think about how the world works: individually, organizationally or collectively. It is a world of perpetual change *and* perpetual transformation.

Creating a culture of continuous transformation, in a world that is itself in flux, requires learning to harness the benefits of constant change and uncertainty, day in and day out. I've been immersed in humans' relationships to change for more than 25 years, and I'd like to share five tips for how to do this:

1) Prioritize mindset before strategy.

There is a great risk that *perpetual transformation* merely finds its way into the *change management* bucket. We must make sure that does not happen. Why? Because change management, while helpful, is incomplete. Let me explain.

All too often, humans get their relationships to change backwards. We focus on developing change management strategies and worry about investing in uncertainty. But what we often fail to remember — or even realize sometimes — is that every single strategy, investment and decision you make is fundamentally rooted in your mindset. Consider:

- Do you see change from a place of hope, or fear? That's not strategy; that's mindset.
- Do you believe you can control your future, and then struggle when things don't go to plan? That's not strategy; that's mindset.

And this isn't just about you. How would your colleagues, team members, friends, and family members answer these questions? In my experience, the answer is: *not* the same way that you do. Everyone's relationship to change is different, because everyone's lived experience is different. We bring different lenses and emotions to the table. And yet, when we make management and strategic decisions, we often assume that others think like we do. Then we wonder why strategies don't go to plan... but the answer is clear: Because we've put the cart before the horse.

Mindset drives strategy, not the other way around.

Strategy doesn't happen in a vacuum. It is shaped by the emotions, assumptions, and quirks that filter and shape how we see the world. Get clear on these and factor them in from the outset. Open what I call a Flux Mindset (and keep reading). You'll see a world of change in a whole new light *and* open yourself up to a much easier, smoother path to perpetual transformation.

2) Open a Flux Mindset.

A Flux Mindset is one's ability to see change consistently as an opportunity, not a threat, and to take advantage of it. It's the ability to see *every change* — loved or hated, small or large, expected or unexpected, welcome or unwanted — as an opportunity to do things better. Having a Flux Mindset doesn't mean merely accepting change, but rather, developing an eagerness to *harness* it well.

A Flux Mindset isn't a magic wand that — poof! — makes unwelcome change disappear. Rather, it is a mental muscle that's grooved to not resist change, nor does it delude you about change or that somehow you're above change. Rather, a Flux Mindset treats constant change and uncertainty as a feature, not a bug — and empowers you to lean into life on that basis.

A Flux Mindset also knows how to answer the question: **What makes you, you — *even when everything else changes?***

The word *flux* is both a noun and a verb. As a noun, it means continuous change or movement. As a verb, it means *to learn to become fluid.* So in a world *in flux*, people and organizations must learn how to *flux*. Enter a Flux Mindset.

Keep in mind, both individuals and organizations can develop Flux Mindsets. At an organizational level, fluxiness becomes an essential element of organizational culture. *What makes your organization — unique and resilient — even when everything else changes?* Hint: This goes far beyond quarterly earnings, marketing pitches, or even customer loyalty. It touches upon company values, yet goes deeper. This gets to the heart of why your company or organization exists in the first place — and whether that stands up to the reality of a world in flux.

Today, how would you rate your organization's ability to flux? Are certain topics trigger points? Are select people, teams, or departments more capable and comfortable embracing change than others?

If you've never thought about these questions, that's already a helpful signal — and a great place to start.

Moving forward, organizations that can flux will be better positioned not only to navigate constant change, but to harness perpetual transformation. In fact, perpetual transformation will be part of their cultural DNA.

3) Reset your relationship to control.

On the whole, humans tend to love changes that we opt into: a new relationship, a new job, a new adventure, even a new song to listen to or a new food to taste. But we tend to really struggle with change that we don't control: the kind of change that blindsides you on a Tuesday afternoon, that goes against your expectations, or that disrupts your plans. We fear these changes, we resist them, and we mistakenly believe we can control them.

What's more, technology often exacerbates this situation. The more devices we have in our pockets — or the more apps on any given device — the more we tend to buy into the belief that we can control what happens next.

A change in location or traffic? GPS will solve that. A change in financial markets? A trading app can fix that. Meeting change? No problem, your calendar app is at the ready. A change in your refrigerator, and ran out of milk? An instant delivery app and you're good to go.

Granted, these are tiny changes in the grand scheme of things. But bit by bit, they lead us to believe that technology somehow has the answer. And yet, when change *really hits* — when the future is uncertain, when the world flips upside-down, when things don't go to plan — nothing could be further from the truth. We wake up to the reality that neither you nor I nor anyone has ever been able to control the future: whether that future is this afternoon, next week, or a decade or century from now. What we're after is merely the *illusion* of control.

Sure, GPS can help us navigate across town. But it will never be able to navigate life. Only you can do that, for your own life, which brings us back to the same question: *What makes you, you — even when everything else changes?* Moreover, in a world of certain uncertainty, what does control even mean?

A Flux Mindset sees through this illusion of control of external circumstances and the outside world, and it shifts its focus to what you can control: how you respond. No one can control a specific outcome, but you *can* control whether and how you contribute to an outcome you'd like to see. No one can predict *the* future, but you can prepare for many different *possible* futures.

This shift — from predict to prepare — is an essential piece of the perpetual transformation puzzle. In fact, this is what perpetual transformation is all about. Reassessing and resetting your relationship to control is key to your ability to deliver on it.

Scenario mapping (or scenario planning) is one powerful tool that can help power a shift from predict to prepare. The purpose of scenario mapping is to shift away from getting fixated on any one particular result that *must* happen, and toward a wide range of outcomes that *may* happen. The scenario mapping process does exactly that: imagining and mapping out as many different possibilities as you can, from amazing to apocalyptic and myriad others in between.

As Winston Churchill said, "Plans are of little importance, but *planning* is essential." The point of scenario planning is not that any one scenario will actually happen (and typically, none do) however what often does happen is that some combination of factors and events that were part of different scenarios comes to bear. Because you've already imagined these possible realities, you're not caught off-guard. You're better able to respond, and you might even find a sense of peace.

4) Reframe the Chief Transformation Officer role.

Chief Transformation Officer is a peculiar and often ill-fitting title. On the one hand, it shows up in organizational charts from time to time, most often in the context of digital transformation: this person is tasked with overseeing a company's shift to digital business operations, services, online presence and the ripple effects (operational, financial, cultural, technological and otherwise) that entails. On the other hand, a range of other CXOs are expected to add transformation to their respective portfolios and domains. CEOs, COOs, CHROs, CTOs, Chief Innovation Officers, Chief Insights Officers, and Chief Culture Officers: all of these are part transformation officer, too — though you would be hard-pressed to find a common definition among their roles. Worst of all, some companies appoint a Chief Transformation Officer in what amounts to little more than a marketing stint.

But in a world in flux, the role of a Chief Transformation Officer takes on new meaning *and* new urgency. When change is rattling and whipsawing organizations every day — from top to bottom, in-person and virtually, from executives to new joiners and everyone in between — a Chief Transformation Officer can no longer be defined in relation to how other roles are changing, nor defined to one function, department, project, or end goal.

To achieve continuous transformation, it's time to rethink and overhaul the Chief Transformation Officer role in two ways: first, with a cross-functional Change Navigation role that addresses the pervasive, relentless change and uncertainty in the world at large and, second, toward adopting *change navigator* status at all levels of the organization, helping all talent strengthen their change muscle (that is, open a Flux Mindset) and ultimately embedding this within organizational culture.

5) Remember: Moving forward, there is no steady state, and no end game other than change. Perpetual transformation is the future.

This is a huge break from what we're often taught *and* how organizations typically operate. That said, *if* we can get comfortable with it, a whole new universe — new opportunities, new ways of building and leading business, new ways of *being* — open up.

By and large, most people are taught that when we reach a certain goal or milestone, you'll be rewarded: for example, that you'll have made it once you've earned a certain amount of money, or that you'll be happy when you've tackled a certain problem. Organizations often exacerbate this: from climbing the corporate ladder rung-by-rung, to our obsession with productivity and more.

Yet, for example, in our quest for productivity, do we stop and ask: Productive *to what end*? Productive *for whom*?

Having more meetings in a given day does not make you more productive, if the meetings themselves are void of meaning. A CEO who asks his or her direct reports to be more productive accomplishes very little if that talent is overworked, burning out, without meaning, or resents being micromanaged in the first place.

Moreover, this way of thinking — that productivity is inherently good, or that more is inherently better — keeps people stuck in a cycle of insufficiency, unhappiness, and wondering: Isn't there more to life? (To be clear: I am not saying don't have dreams and goals and strive to be happy. But keep in mind: *There is no end point after which happiness, or success, or certainty is guaranteed. All of these things will themselves change… and this* is what we need to get radically and completely comfortable with.)

Ironically, it's usually when change hits — when a window for transformation appears — that these disconnects are most acutely felt. So part of the answer of how to deliver on perpetual transformation is to ask these questions: Productive *for what end*? Productive *for whom*? Is more better, or is enough, enough? — on a continuous, daily basis. *This* is how you create cultures where transformation is always underway.

Coming full circle, the pace of change has never been as fast as it is today, yet it is likely to never again be this slow. This reality isn't about a pandemic, or any one change, or any one year. *The future is in flux.* The new-now-next-never normal is more constant change, not more certainty or stability. Against this backdrop, the five steps highlighted above represent a sea change in how we think about, talk about, relate to, lead through, and ultimately thrive in perpetual transformation. Only by reshaping our relationships to change and uncertainty — individually and collectively — will we be able to build, grow, and lead fluxy organizations and forge a brighter future for all.

About the author

A World Economic Forum Young Global Leader and ranked one of the "50 Leading Female Futurists" by *Forbes*, **April Rinne** is a change navigator: she helps individuals and organizations rethink and reshape their relationship with change, uncertainty, and a world in flux. She is a trusted advisor to well-known startups, companies, financial institutions, nonprofits, and think tanks worldwide, including Airbnb, Nike, Intuit, the World Bank, the Inter-American Development Bank, NESTA, Trōv, AnyRoad, and Unsettled, as well as governments ranging from Singapore to South Africa, Canada to Colombia, Italy to India. April is the author of *Flux: 8 Superpowers for Thriving in Constant Change* (Berrett-Koehler, 2021).

A graduate of Harvard Law School, April has been weaving a story about how to thrive amid flux for as long as she can remember, drawing on her history as a futurist, advisor, global development executive, microfinance lawyer, investor, mental health advocate, certified yoga teacher, globetrotter (100+ countries), and insatiable handstander. April also harnesses her very personal experiences with flux, including the death of both of her parents in a car accident when she was 20. Through her travels and tragedy, vision and values, global perspective and grounded sense of purpose, April helps others better understand how we see, think about, struggle with, and ultimately forge positive relationships with change. More at fluxmindset.com.

Becoming a focused organization to achieve perpetual transformation

ANTONIO NIETO-RODRIGUEZ

17

In his 1962 book *Strategy and Structure*, Alfred Chandler argues that an organization's structure should be driven by its chosen strategy and that, if it isn't, inefficiency results.[101]

Taking this one step further, the degree to which project activities are reflected in the organization's structure determines overall implementation success. When executives underestimate or completely ignore this fact, organizations fail to evolve (or adapt) as quickly as the business and markets do. As a result, organizations disappear and a large proportion of strategic projects fail.

Having the right organizational and governing structure is probably the biggest challenge of achieving perpetual transformation. Making changes within an organization is extremely complicated for two fundamental reasons: those that pertain to history and those relating to human behavior. First, organizations are built over many years; and over time, they become rusty, expensive to run, and out of touch with reality. Second, the hundreds and sometimes thousands of individuals that make up an organization have their old habits, which they are often reluctant to change. Some of these individuals are also influenced by decision-making power, which is often reflected by who has the largest department, the highest budgets, and the biggest salary.

Most Western companies have a functional or hierarchical structure. The theory behind hierarchy aims at efficiency and specialization. This was ideal for running the business efficiently in a stable world. Departments are divided along a value chain influenced by Michael Porter's value chain model.[102] Traditional companies are generally run by a CEO, a CFO, and often a COO and a CIO, followed by the heads of business units and functional departments. Each has their own budget, resources, objectives and priorities. Hierarchical organizations consolidate information and control on a few people at the top of the company, where all the information comes together. The most essential and strategic decisions are taken by the leading group, often slowly and far removed from the market reality.

What today's organizations really need is a strategy to help people make the decisions. Organizations need the agility to react at the level of where things are actually happening, which is typically at the operating level.

In addition, until recently, departmental success was measured using key performance indicators tailored to each unit or function. For example, the finance department's success was measured by whether it was closing the books and producing the financial statements on time, and the HR department's by whether it had managed to keep good people on board (low turnover) or had finished employee appraisals on time.

A few heads of units tend to establish their own territories, and collaboration across different parts of the business is often troublesome. To the point that it is not unusual to have conflicting performance indicators between departments.

On the other hand, the most critical transformations, the most strategic ones, are of transversal — company-wide — nature. They require resources, time and budgets from every single department in the organization. Without the commitment and contribution of everyone, it is most likely that the transformation will not succeed.

Cross-departmental — or company-wide — transformations in a traditional functional organization always face the same difficulties, some of which are linked to the following questions:

- Which department is going to lead the transformation?
- Who is going to be the project manager?
- Who is the sponsor of the transformation?
- Who is rewarded if the transformation is successful?
- Who is the owner of the resources assigned to the transformation?
- Who is going to pay for the transformation?

The silo mentality adds to this complexity, with managers often wondering why they should commit resources and a budget to a project that, although important, would not give them any credit if successful. Rather, a management colleague, often a direct competitor, would benefit.

Within the traditional organization, transformation is cumbersome. Managing just one strategic initiative in such a complex structure is a challenge, so imagine the difficulty of trying to achieve perpetual transformation; impossible.

Creating a culture where transformation is fostered

A company's successful transformation depends not only on whether the company performs well. A successful company also achieves sustainable growth of both revenues and profits; consistently delivers its strategy; outperforms the competition; is viewed as a market leader and has fulfilled staff.

One of the outcomes of my research was that these successful organizations in a world driven by change were not just reaching but were also exceeding their strategic objectives. Although having a great leader, a well-known brand, and a very good product or service contributed to this success, what made all the difference in their ability to surpass their expectations and create an organization where transformation is always underway was the fact that they were FOCUSED.

To better explain the key elements, a company needs to be successful in a world driven by change, and to put transformation at the center, I turned the word FOCUSED into an acronym that stands for:

F — Fewer projects, rather than many. A focused organization that can effectively select and prioritize its transformation projects and invest in just one or two good initiatives at a time clearly outperforms organizations that take on too many projects. The few projects that are selected are linked to one or several strategic objectives and are fully supported by top management.

It is fundamental that these few initiatives are communicated and understood by the entire organization. The chance of having the organization understand and remember three transformative initiatives is higher than if the company were faced with multiple initiatives. Also, because only two or three strategic projects are selected each year, management is forced to find the best ideas. Transformation projects require full management attention, and to carry out more than three almost guarantees failure.

O — Organized staff. In a focused enterprise, the staff is organized in such a way that all personnel know what is expected of them and are recognized for their contribution. They do not waste time on activities that are not part of their core skill set; rather, they focus on their key strengths and core capabilities instead of trying all the time to improve their weaknesses.

Top management monitors the execution of these transformation and strategic projects at least monthly and follows through until the projects are completed, the benefits are delivered and the transformation is achieved. They have to split their time between change, managerial activities, participating as project sponsors, attending project steering committees, and dealing with day-to-day operational activities such as sales meetings. Because they have set the business's priorities, they know how to distribute their time most effectively.

C — Competitive mindset. A focused organization competes with the outside world rather than internally. Internal competition, which might be good in the short term, but negative in the long term, is eliminated because all the organization's effort is placed on doing what it does best. The CEO and top management explicitly identify rival organizations, often referring to them in their speeches and communications to the company.

The focused company is also very clear about how to beat the competition. In fact, there is only one way: creating better products and delivering better services. A high degree of innovation is a key and common characteristic of a focused organization.

In addition, the employees of such companies tend to have winning attitudes. They are talented and ambitious and want to progress in their careers. Unlike employees in unfocused organizations, they do not compete with their fellow employees because the focus on outside forces is so strong.

Examples of this external competition exist in almost every industry: Windows versus Mac; Google versus Yahoo; Facebook versus LinkedIn; Shell versus BP; HP versus Dell; Boeing versus Airbus; and many others. With today's extreme globalization, competition comes not only from the same industry, but from different industries. For example, Microsoft competes with both Apple and Google.

U — Urgency. In a world driven by change, time is money. Organizations need to launch their transformation initiatives quickly. The time-to-market for new products must become shorter and shorter. Creating a sense of urgency is a competitive advantage, and the focused organization is always aware of this fact. Urgency is also needed to focus people and encourage them to give their best performance.

Ensuring that employees are very familiar with the key strategic projects selected by top management helps to build this sense of urgency. Employees know that they cannot postpone their work and that they must deliver on time what is expected from them.

Clear deadlines, fixed goals and knowledge of the importance (and the benefits) of each strategic project are tools with which to infuse the entire organization, both management and staff, with urgency and focus. These techniques also provide the sense that things are moving faster, almost as if the tempo at which the company usually works is doubled or tripled. People work harder; the tempo seems faster, and results are achieved more quickly. This sense of urgency can be achieved in both the run-the-business and the change-the-business dimensions. However, pressure can be applied more strongly to the change-the-business side, which would then serve as a driver for activities in the rest of the organization.

One point to consider, and a real warning for top management, is the need to impose the sense of urgency carefully. If management and staff are pushed too hard for too long, they will not be able to cope with the pace and will burn out. A collateral issue is that when pushed too hard to perform, people tend to take higher risks than normal. At first, this behavior may pay off; but in the long term, it is not sustainable. In addition, management and staff may find ways to produce exceptional results without following the "rules." Both scenarios often have disastrous consequences for the organizations.

In 2005, a new CEO arrived at one of Belgium's leading banks, with a mission to grow the bank internationally and bring it into the European Ivy League of Banks. He created focus by setting two clear targets: first, to increase the benefit per share by at least 10 percent between 2005 and 2009; second, to double the profit coming from outside Benelux from 15 percent in 2004 to 30 percent. He also introduced a few strategic initiatives that would help achieve these targets. Beginning with his management team, the new CEO quickly increased the focus and the pressure in the entire organization.

This approach worked for three years, with the organization moving faster and faster and targets being met. One of the CEO's strategic initiatives was to buy a small bank in the US to build and sell in the subprime market. At the same time, an opportunity arose to join a consortium of leading banks, Royal Bank of Scotland and Banco Santander, to buy one of the leading banks in the world, the Dutch ABN Amro.

With two very strategic projects immediately following a couple of years of aggressive focus and pressure, management and most of the staff were exhausted. The organization could not cope; and with the collapse of the financial market, the bank went into bankruptcy.

This is probably the most important risk of a focused organization and perpetual transformation: Putting too much pressure for too long on the staff and the organization — what I refer to as aggressive focus — can bring amazing short-term results but in the long term is not sustainable.

S — Strategic alignment. Every transformative project in a focused organization should be linked to one or several strategic objectives. Any initiative that is not so linked should be immediately cancelled. This alignment is necessary to ensure that the company achieves its stated goals.

Having only a few key transformative projects is the best contribution to strategy achievement. For example, recently a consumer goods producer decided to acquire a company in China that built and sold ironing machines. This project was perfectly aligned with the company's strategy, which was to have a presence in China and to increase profits coming from that region by 20 percent. The company successfully acquired and integrated the Chinese plant, which immediately provided a 30 percent profit coming from the Asian region.

E — Excellence. A focused organization applies the highest standards to everything it does, and its products and/or services are known for their quality. Sustainable excellence requires attention to the details of every aspect of the organization: values, quality of employees, internal and external processes, products, and customer service.

The key strategic initiatives are managed by and staffed with the most capable people. Both the project sponsor and the project team are selected based on which employees throughout the organization will be the best at driving the initiative. This approach leaves little room for internal politics.

D — Discipline. Companies today need discipline to execute their key initiatives; without it, consistent performance becomes very difficult and perpetual transformation fails.

Discipline is defined as *"training to act in accordance with rules"* or *"the activity, exercise or regimen that develops or improves a skill."* It requires practice and helps organizations to quickly react and perform. One of the most disciplined organizations, the army, would not be able to carry out its defense programs without discipline.

Discipline should not be seen as something negative that inhibits innovation. Rather, innovation depends on discipline. Companies should clearly distinguish between the time set aside for creativity and time allocated to implementation. Focused organizations can make this distinction and move from the creative phase to the execution phase very quickly. If companies spend too much on innovation, they will be too late by the time they decide to execute their strategy. The challenge for the CEO and the company's entire management team is to find the right balance between discipline and creativity/flexibility.

Discipline for the staff means that once the strategic project has been approved by top management, it should be meticulously executed without being questioned again and again. This does not mean that there is no room for discussion, especially if the project faces unexpected issues during the design or implementation phase; but the project selection should not be further debated.

One final, and very important, aspect of discipline in a focused organization is that required by the CEO and top management when waiting to see results. Many of the benefits of transformations are not seen until the medium to long term, and management must be patient to achieve the bigger results. Too much pressure on short-term results will eventually be harmful.

The benefits of becoming a focused organization

The benefits of becoming a focused organization are significant, the most important being:

Achieve strategic goals. Everybody in the focused organization, from the CEO to the accounts payable employee, knows the direction in which the organization is going, why perpetual transformation is vital, which two to three initiatives are the most important for that year, and the purpose for these few critical initiatives.

Attain financial and value creation results. Positive financial and value creation results are a direct consequence of achieving the company's strategy. In the end it is probably the most important benefit of becoming a focused organization, since organizations need to have good results to survive and to provide a good return to their shareholders.

The benefits of becoming focused can be significant and the results can appear very quickly on the company's bottom line, particularly on the cost side. Costs are reduced when irrelevant projects are canceled, which can add up to huge savings. Between 40 to 50 percent of projects could be easily canceled without any major impact, which in turn frees up budgets and resources to execute key strategic projects.

Become a high-performing organization. Because a focused organization is clearly organized, allocates its employees to those positions at which they are best, and clearly defines it goals, it becomes a high-performing organization. It is not just a team that is high performing, which can be the case in a very strategic project; it is the entire organization.

A high-performing team is characterized by a feeling of magic to the members. The sum of the team of people can achieve far more than the sum of the individual's skills alone — "A high-performing team is a small number of people with complementary skills who are committed to a common purpose, performance goals, and approach for which they hold themselves mutually accountable."[103]

My experience is a high-performing team is rare. But when it happens, all members give their best, work hard, are committed, do not engage in internal competition, and are happy and feel proud to belong to that team. The same is true of a focused — high-performing — organization: Employees are happy to work there, are very strongly committed, and are proud to show that they work at such a good company. Obviously, all these benefits turn into one large benefit for the organization: successful strategy execution and improved financial results.

Develop a winning culture that embraces transformation. Today, many organizations love to discuss new business initiatives, especially in lengthy meetings; but they stop at the discussion stage. Alternatively, companies start initiatives and after a few months resume arguing about decisions made in the past. Progress is very slow, and the initiatives' momentum is killed.

A focused organization selects just a few transformative initiatives and gets them done before starting new ones. Once an initiative has been chosen, all the company's focus is on execution. Results are shown in short time frames, and progress is monitored according to plan. Building momentum is very important when creating a culture of getting things done, and the CEO and top management need to lead by example.

Build a happy, committed, and engaged workforce. The last major benefit of a focused organization is that its employees are satisfied and have a positive sense of accomplishment despite being in constant transformation. They work in the position they are best at and that adds the most value to the organization, and they like what they do as opposed to just performing a job.

Today every organization, public or private, operates in an environment subject to continual and sometimes disruptive levels of change. This extreme uncertainty generates a difficult operating environment for leaders and organizations. The yearly cycle that worked for almost a century no longer applies. The radically transformed circumstances call for new ways of working, more-agile and focused operating models, and new forms of leadership. Organizational structures, processes, and systems need to be adapted, too, to ensure the perpetual transformation of the organization and to take advantage of new opportunities brought by the deeply changeable world, also known as the Project Economy.

About the author

Antonio Nieto-Rodriguez is a leading expert in project management and strategy implementation, recognized by Thinkers50 with its Ideas into Practice Award. He is the author of the *Harvard Business Review Project Management Handbook* and four other books. The former chairman of the Project Management Institute, he is the founder of Projects & Co and co-founder of the Strategy Implementation Institute. Antonio has been teaching project management for more than a decade to senior executives at Duke CE, Skolkovo, Solvay Business School, and Vlerick. He has held executive positions at PricewaterhouseCoopers, BNP Paribas, and GlaxoSmithKline.

Footnotes

101 Alfred Chandler, *Strategy and Structure: Chapters in the History of the Industrial Enterprise* (Cambridge, MA: MIT Press, 1962).

102 "Porter's Value Chain" (IfM), accessed 2 October 2018, https://www.ifm.eng.cam.ac.uk/research/dstools/value-chain-.

103 Jon Katzenbach and Douglas Smith, *The Wisdom of Teams* (Harvard Business School Press, 1993).

A paradigm shift for managers: Focus on the journey, not the destination

GABRIELE ROSANI AND PAOLO CERVINI

18

Managing change has always been part of the leadership toolkit. Shifts in markets and industries require strategy and product repositioning with implications for organizations and processes. Although challenging, change has traditionally been perceived as something manageable. With the right tools in place — a thorough analysis of the root causes, a structured definition of the expected future state, and a detailed plan for implementation — the organization can navigate the tides of change.

Take the case of a newly appointed CEO announcing a transformation initiative with a new strategy and organizational redesign. The CEO could once rely on a well-established theory of change based on three stages: unfreeze, change, refreeze. Within this theory, classic management tools like Gantt charts, RACI (Responsible, Accountable, Consulted, or Informed) matrices, organizational diagrams, and KPIs (key performance indicators) helped implement and monitor the change. But this is no longer the case.

A traditional approach was only effective in situations where change happened as a discrete event. It offered a process to facilitate the transition from one stable condition to another, not a continuous flow. However, in today's economy, change is perpetual and ubiquitous: there is no such thing as unfreeze or refreeze; the transformation is ongoing and fluid. Consequently, most of the frameworks and tools that might have worked in the past now fall short.

The implications for management are enormous. Strategy formulation and planning require high fluidity to cope with dynamic ecosystems and disruptive trends. Digitalization drives a continuous release of products and calls for high flexibility and adaptability of processes. Organizations continually evolve toward more liquid and agile shapes. Decision making and control systems need to foster empowerment and reduce bureaucracy.

Executives may find themselves with little support for such daunting challenges. In our work as consultants, we often hear requests from clients for new frameworks and tools to simply replace the old ones that no longer work. We believe there's something fundamentally wrong with this mindset.

The very notion of management tools needs to be rethought. Tools tend to be static, mechanical, biased, and prescriptive. They are static because they simplify a complex and dynamic context into a fixed reality; mechanical because they are often applied without real thought and discussion to derive a formulaic solution; classic tools like spreadsheets or linear charts are also often biased as they favor the status quo, mistakenly relying on buried assumptions that remain unchallenged; and, finally, they are prescriptive, limiting the freedom and good judgment of managers who feel they are bound by a given structure and rules.

Today, rather than a new toolkit, managers need a new mental model to navigate the transformative journey, one that is essentially more explorative and experimental. Such a shift is not easy as it demands that we unlearn most of the traditional tools entrenched in management practices, and try relatively untested new approaches, offering guidelines rather than well-honed tools.

Leveraging our recent research and projects, we have experimented with new approaches to deal with perpetual transformations covering several important management fields: from strategy to organization to processes (summarized in the table below).

Elements of management	Traditional tools	New approaches
Strategy formulation	Market analysis/ positioning	Evolving ecosystem
Strategy implementation	Detailed plan (Gantt, work-breakdown structure)	Learning experiments
Decision making & control	Preventive control model	Empowering control models
Organizational design	Boxes and lines, RACI	Team-based agile circles
Culture & leadership	Manifesto (value statement)	Behaviors in action
Change management	3 stages (unfreeze, change, refreeze)	Continuous releases ('versions')

Strategy formulation

In a more stable past, it was normal to hear managers saying: this is my industry, this is my product segment, these are my competitors, this is the value chain. Today these simple notions are becoming problematic. The boundaries between sectors are becoming increasingly blurred, so these traditional lenses of stability are of little help to navigate the new landscape. A more systemic view is required.

We advise strategists to shift from *market* thinking to *ecosystem* thinking.

The ecosystem, as the name suggests, is a living system that evolves continuously depending not only on the moves of any individual organism but also on the ones made by all the other organisms that coexist with it. This creates an evolutionary direction of change that is hard to predict due to the complexity of the whole system. Companies in different sectors from Enel (utilities) to DBS (banking), to John Deere (agriculture), to Haier (smart appliances) have already shifted their strategy formulation toward an ecosystem approach. Instead of focusing on the *As-Is* analysis, benchmarking competitors, to derive a *To-Be* positioning, this approach fosters creativity around a few strategic hypotheses and scenarios generating a *Could-Be* view of the world.

Strategy implementation

Used for planning implementation and monitoring, the ubiquitous Gantt chart is perhaps the most used (and abused) tool in management. Geared as it is to transforming *As-Is* thinking into *To-Be* solutions, it can be toxic in situations of continuous change and perpetual transformation (*Could-Be*). We recommend that strategists and executives embrace a more fluid and experimental approach when implementing strategy. Rather than a plan of detailed initiatives, managers should list the main strategic hypotheses of the *Could-Be* and articulate what to test and how to test via learning experiments. Insights and evidence from these experiments will bring learnings and iterations on the original strategic scenarios.

For example, a specialty chemical company we worked with envisioned two different ecosystems for its paint additives business. The company rapidly tested the strategic assumptions for both: the first one (initially the favorite) found negative evidence from potential partners, while the second scenario, partly due to the consumer shift caused by COVID-19, proved more favorable and quickly became prioritized.

Decision making and control

Where there is a Gantt chart, typically there are also gates and steering committees, to vet and make formal decisions. Gates and steering committees are among the most critical barriers for companies in a scenario of perpetual transformation: the intrinsic linearity, hierarchy, slowness, and inflexibility they represent makes them unfit for continuous change. But cracking the system is possible. Some pioneers like Netflix and Handelsbanken are paving the way for shifting from the traditional preventive control to new models (like post-detection, guiding principles, boundary conditions, peer review, sounding board, social control, etc.) to free up the energy and the imagination of the organization without losing control.

The new set of decision making and control models are helpful when rethinking critical processes in a more fluid way. Rather than reengineering the processes (an approach which is itself intrinsically heavy and bureaucratic), we advise executives to try a different mental scheme, one that is more creative and experimental. Look at the big picture and identify key decision points where new control models can be applied — and then test them with small learning pilots. For example, a large utility company rethought its business development process to fit an increasingly dynamic ecosystem, shifting from traditional stage gates and steering committees to a more agile and empowered model with ample autonomy within clear guidelines, peer pressure and boundary conditions.

Organizational design

Organizational charts that use boxes and lines to represent the organization in a pyramid shape are also popular tools of traditional management. Again, this mental model of organizations is unfit for today's world. Even though many companies claim to be adopting more agile approaches, in most cases the organizational chart retains its traditional design. However, if agile teams are surrounded by hierarchical and functional structures that maintain power, budget, and decision making, only a limited fraction of the agile potential can be unleashed. In our experience, few firms have truly embraced a model of organizational agility based on autonomous multidisciplinary teams as the core unit of their organization. Yet, companies like Bosch, Roche, and Haier, each with its own style and culture, have shown that a fully agile transformation is possible and brings significant benefits.

Culture and leadership

Another stereotype of traditional management is the manifesto or value statement. The manifesto may change from time to time, typically in conjunction with important organizational transformations when new values are needed to match the new strategy. One of the problems with such an approach is that values can often appear to be abstract. They offer a statement of good intent, not an action.

Rather than defining vague values communicated on posters in the corridors, leaders should agree on a set of concrete behaviors they want their people to adopt (or behaviors they want them to stop), which are valid for the current situation. We call this approach 'behaviors in action,' following a principle of dynamic adjustment to the real circumstances of business. This approach was applied, for example, at a major pharmaceutical company. The leadership decided to focus on candor and collaboration as key elements to promote an innovative and transformational culture, not as abstract values but by identifying a set of specific behaviors for different layers of management, which are periodically reviewed and discussed in retrospective sessions.

Change management

In perpetual transformation, change is no more an episode happening between two long periods of relative stability. In such an environment, change is the normal condition. The question is how to deal with a situation where the company is always unfreezing and never really refreezing, where the onus is on remaining liquid and only some blocks being refrozen. So, how can a company exist in a semi-liquid state, where it is always mutating and reshaping?

In practice, we suggest organizing project outputs as continual releases of 'versions' of the organization that are constantly evolving: some versions may change often, other may last longer, some may even be terminated. The focus is on the journey and how the versions unfold.

One of our clients, an advanced materials company based in the U.S., wanted to rethink its new product development approach to make it more fluid, fast and agile. Rather than designing a To-Be state, the company identified a combination of three solutions as *version 1.0* to be tested. Gantt charts were banned, and all the effort was put into articulating and testing a few core assumptions. As evidence became available through talking with customers and partners, initial versions evolved and in some parts were pivoted. Underpinning this approach was a shift in mindset, whereby the company does not plan to refreeze the new process and make it stable, but they will continue to revise versions over time. The result is a sort of living change process.

Perpetual transformation is the new normal for business. It appears to be a daunting challenge for executives as old-school tools do not fit well and sometimes are even counterproductive, limiting strategic creativity, freedom and flexibility.

To help managers shift paradigm we advocate the use of radically different approaches in key areas of management, from strategy formulation to processes and organization. The proposed approaches are evolutionary and iterative in nature, following the transformative journey as it evolves. The experimental condition is a fundamental part of the mindset shift. To thrive in a world of perpetual transformation, managers should stop thinking and acting prescriptively, and rather embrace a liquid style, where adopting a systemic view, hypotheses, experimentation, testing and learning become the new core of management.

About the authors

Gabriele Rosani is a senior manager at ECSI Consulting.
Paolo Cervini is an associate partner at ECSI Consulting.

Change vitality:
How to lead for
continual
transformation

DEBORAH ROWLAND

19

Twenty years ago, I launched what has now become a regular cycle of empirical research into what it takes to lead big complex change well. The initial research inquiry, Is Change Changing? carried two questions. On the cusp of the new millennium and dawn of a digital, globally interconnected age, was the nature of change itself — and how to lead it — changing? But more than that, by simply inserting a comma between the two words, 'change' and 'changing,' could we replace the notion of change as a singular event with its recognition as a continual state of being?

Perpetual transformation is no new concept. It was 2500 years ago that Greek philosopher Heraclitus notably proclaimed, "nothing endures but change."[104] But fast-forward to two decades ago and what fueled my initial research were management thinkers such as Pascale[105] and Senge[106] placing the notion of change as a constant state in the forefront of a leader's mind. And today, undoubtedly amplified by 18 months of ducking and diving the uncertain waves of COVID-19, perpetual transformation is a deeply lived reality. The question stands before us — have our leadership practices and approach to change caught up with this dawning reality?

In this article, I share a holistic framework, Change Vitality,[107] that I and my colleagues have created to guide leaders through the navigation of constant change. Grounded in now four rounds of research over two decades, Change Vitality stands on the shoulders of hundreds of leaders across all continents, industries and sectors who have generously given their time to participate in in-depth behavioral event interviews that we rigorously code for what leads to success in a continually changing world. I hope the framework guides you too.

Introducing Change Vitality

Perpetual transformation calls for a distinct new way to lead change. One that replaces notions of launching time-bound, system-wide, centrally controlled 'change programs' with the subtler realization that ongoing change is an inherent feature of all living systems[108] — and that if we could only understand how change naturally occurs, we could lead it with less busy effort and more easeful impact — a distinction I call the difference between 'action' and 'movement.'[109]

A key tenet, therefore, of Change Vitality is that *you only do what is necessary* (vital). Change is also not something you periodically *bring* to a system, separate to its task, but an ongoing phenomenon you inherently *cultivate* — continually pausing (stillness) in the flow of work to scan your team, organization and wider context for the ripe issues that most need attention, and in these spots targeting minimally invasive experiments that have enduring, energetic, whole system impact (movement).[110]

As such, I liken Change Vitality to 'corporate acupuncture' — as distinct from 'corporate surgery.' Witness how with one client I worked with, the simple and singular act of training meeting observers to continually spot and name in-the-moment decision-making routines sped up cultural change in a way their elaborate "new ways of working" programs and governance redesigns could never have achieved.

Change Vitality therefore requires you to go *to the source* of the system's routines and regularly hold that up to attention (a bit like doing a daily body scan for your physical well-being).[111] In the above example the inner code was "we cannot make a collective decision until everyone is happy with the decision so we will spend as much time as we need trying to accommodate everyone to a compromise." When the pleasing culture got named, change could occur.

So, how to cultivate this ongoing, system-shifting Change Vitality? While more effortless, it is not without effort!

The Still Moving Change Vitality Framework

Our research has revealed four essential, richly interdependent factors that, together, enable leaders to cultivate successful Change Vitality:

- *Inner Capacities:* the quality of your inner state as a leader, how people experience your *being*
- *External Practices:* the effectiveness of your outer behavior, what people will see you *doing*
- *Change Approach:* how you choose overall to design and implement change across the system you lead
- *Ordering Forces:* how you attend to the deeper systemic health of your organization that governs how your change will either flow or get stuck.

It's a lot to pay attention to — hardly surprising that most change efforts fail.[112] But when you *do* take this 'how' of change seriously, you have a far higher chance of success. Given the high price of change and the toll it takes on people's time, energy and lives, set alongside the prize it can bring to markets, societies, livelihoods — indeed our very planet's survival — I feel this is an effort worth taking.

Still Moving Change Vitality Cone

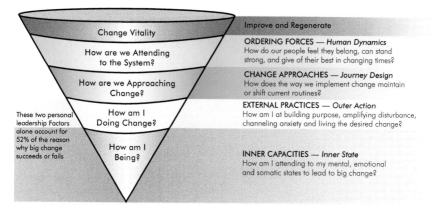

© Still Moving Consultancy Ltd

We visualize the four Change Vitality factors as a flow of energy that rises upward through a spinning cone. Perpetual change can feel like this — a bit wobbly, risky, hard to stay in balance. And we all know that the essence of the cone's ability to move at pace, yet remain stable, rests on how securely it pivots on the ground. The Inner Capacities are at the bottom of the cone for a reason. The startling, primary message from our research is this:[113]

Your entire ability to lead whole systems through perpetual change rests on how well you cultivate your inner state, your ability to tune into and regulate your mental and emotional response to experience.

Change Vitality starts in the quality of your being

I never forget the time when I was an executive leading big change and I decided to switch from trying to change the team and process that I was leading, and in its place work on my inner state. It would have been very expensive and time-consuming to change the team and the process, but by flipping my inner state from judgment, impatience and a need to be seen as perfect to curiosity, stillness and an expansive humility — the quality of people's engagement and the speed of the change shifted perceptibly. My inner state altered the outer world.

We cannot always directly control the external world of perpetual motion, as hard as we might try. But we do have the power and freedom to change how we respond to it, and in so doing, get a different world. I danced for joy when my research proved Frankl's[114] wisdom applicable to leading change. The Inner Capacities mediated all other variables. What a pivot your inner world is.

Sounds easy, but our ego can get in the way. To override our neural patterning, our research revealed four Inner Capacities that require your continual attention. Scan this 'to be list' — how well do you intentionally cultivate your quality of being?

- **Staying Present:** the awareness and wisdom that arises from paying intentional nonjudgmental attention to what's here, now, for you — your moods, thoughts, impulses — without mental distraction or wishing for things to be otherwise. There is so much rich data available to us in the present moment — what information does it hold? You cannot change what you don't notice.
- **Curious and Intentional Responding:** the capacity to slow down the period between what you experience and how you respond, staying open and curious to what arises, aware of your choices and intention in how to respond. Switching from autopilot reactivity to creative response shifts the system around you — what fresh leadership mindset can I bring here? Pause permits perspective.
- **Tuning into the System:** when you are present to the moment and free of personal reactivity, you can now more clearly see the deeper dynamics of the system around you, free of your story and projection. This heightened perception capacity into the field that underlies what you see was paramount for successful change leaders. Can you put your finger on what underpins reality and might require transforming?

- **Acknowledging the Whole:** the capacity to give everything that happens a place and a purpose, and in particular, to welcome difficulty and disturbance as a helpful resource for renewal. It's tempting to push away discomfort in change, but what gets excluded only gets bigger. Can you enlarge your leadership and help others integrate all that is encountered, seeing each and every experience as helpful?

Notice, choose, perceive and integrate — your four inner state resources for a world of perpetual motion, and the basis for all else that matters in leading change well.

Perpetual change requires an equal balance of structure and chaos

The Inner Capacities enable you to be calm, resourceful, and systemically alert — a fundamental *being* quality. They enable you to up your game in what you then need to *do* to lead change well. The four External Practices are highly correlated to leading successful change, and when combined enable you to keep a system in continual, creative motion. Drawing from the science of 'complex adaptive systems,'[115] that shows us how such continual innovation holds an equal balance of structure and chaos, the four practices span two axes of stability and disruption.

Stabilizing practices
- *Attractor*: the skill that creates a magnetic, guiding and aligning energy by building a sense of shared purpose and meaning for the change. Can tune into patterns and from these cocreate a compelling narrative that acts as a continual North Star, inspiring others to move into new directions. How are you fueling the change story?
- *Container:* can channel the inevitable anxiety of change into constructive energy by staying nonanxious, affirming, and clear about expectations and boundaries — what has to be done and how. Makes it psychologically safe for people to say/do risky things, builds ownership, and puts in place networks that support people through change. How are you creating secure spaces for movement?

Disrupting practices

- *Edge and Tension:* can shift a system toward a new potential by speaking straight and candidly about reality, ruthlessly focusing only on what matters, spotting and challenging unhelpful assumptions and behaviors, and staying constant, not withdrawing from difficulty, when the going gets tough. Can you get comfortable with amplifying disturbance?
- *Transforming Space:* makes change happen in the here-and-now by creating and making interventions that live (not just talk about) the desired change. This could be changing the nature of a conversation to more fully enact what is being espoused, designing meetings that disrupt routines and enable transforming encounters, or putting together novel mixes of people. Are you being the change you want to see?

The top five percentile of change leaders in our research were able to master all four practices, combining them into powerful, 'multi-hit' interventions. Do you notice your leadership in them? How well do you put them together, do you lean toward some more than others? Are you more of a stabilizer or a disrupter? Putting all four practices together becomes easier once you have mastered the Inner Capacities. Can you start to see the connections between the quality of your 'being' and the skill of your 'doing'? For example, it is very hard to make a Transforming Space intervention if you are not Staying Present.

These first two Change Vitality factors are about your *personal* leadership skill and are paramount. Indeed, our research showed that 52% of the variance between success and failure in high magnitude change is attributed to the quality of a leader's inner state and outer action. But there are two additional Change Vitality factors that require your attention, which relate to how well you create the wider, *systemic* capacity for change. The next factor up the Change Vitality cone is your choice of Change Approach.

Now is the time for an emergence

A Change Approach is the overall way in which you design and implement change. Too often we focus solely on the *what* of a change — for example, do we need to restructure, is a cultural change required? And we fail to pay attention to the *how* of the change, that is, the *process through which* the restructuring will occur, or the cultural change implemented. Yet, our research has shown that your choice of change approach is fateful — it will fundamentally determine where you end up.

One approach in particular — emergent change — was highly correlated with success in ongoing, rapidly changing dynamic contexts. In today's world, heavily engineered top-down approaches to change that assume a fixed destination simply do not work. Here is how we have taken the principles of emergence from complex adaptive systems and applied them to how you approach organizational change:[116]

- *Have a loose direction and set of hard rules.* In perpetual change, you need to give up predetermined visions and control over end points and instead articulate the biggest question that needs answering, or simply set an overall change intention. Then craft some statements of the micro-level behaviors that will govern the pattern of the overall entity — and take it from there. One client we worked with on becoming more 'agile' gave up rolling out agility training programs and instead issued several simple, expected behavioral statements such as "stop when it is good enough," "plan in weeks, not months," "focus on high impact within your control." The understanding and enactment of these few hard rules alone fundamentally shifted the entity's culture and performance and had a catalytic impact on its wider context.
- *Start with the ripe issues.* Don't try to roll out change everywhere, but (by tuning into the system) focus on the hot spots most requiring attention and target where you go. Given that the hot spots can change unpredictably, continually ask: where does the focus need to be now?
- *Work now and next.* When you design for emergent change, you do not plan or predict for the long term but instead test and iterate partially formed solutions step by step — prototyping your way to the future. In rapidly changing contexts, that is the only sensible thing to do, focusing on what is needed and critical now, and from there see what is needed next.
- *Use volunteers and informal networks.* Rapid and creative change happens when you bring together lateral networks of communities passionate about getting involved with the change. Innovation most often happens at the periphery, not center of a system, where diverse contexts are encountered. Memorably, when I was working in the healthcare sector, it was the hospital porters trolleying patients around the buildings that were most able to contribute to improved patient outcomes.

- *Build skills in sensemaking and high-quality dialogue.* When you work in the unfolding flow of emergence, you hold off premature judgment and cultivate moment-to-moment awareness, the approaching of experience with a watchful curiosity, and intervening to alter the flow of action when the time is right. Such penetrating noticing awareness is a high skill indeed. Make sure you focus on how to change how conversations happen.
- *At all times, cultivate the emergent conditions of connectivity, rapid feedback loops and diversity.* While emergent change cannot be controlled, it will flourish naturally if you build into your change high quality interaction spaces among key players and teams, an absolute insistence on open, transparent and rapid information sharing, and the gathering together of a rich cross-section of the whole system.

Harnessing the systemic undercurrents that govern perpetual flow

And so, we arrive at the fourth and final Change Vitality factor: the Ordering Forces. Unlike the first three, the Ordering Forces hold an invariant quality, they are constantly present in any human system.[117] They are not skills to be cultivated or approaches to be brought, but deep hidden forces that govern all collective life. And a bit like the wind, they can be keenly felt while never 'seen.' Smart change leaders act as more than windsocks though. They not only pick up but harness these Ordering Forces, which, if left unattended, will always exert some kind of 'drag' on the change, making things seem like a lot more effort than they need to be.

The four systemic forces are:
- *Time:* all life is governed by time — the residual impact of unalterable past events, a system's creation myth, the positive anticipation of or fear for future events and scenarios. All exert a powerful gravitational pull on the present. Good change leaders recognize we cannot move freely into new futures until all important past elements have been seen — even if that creates felt guilt and shame. In addition to exploring a system's history, good change leaders tune into how the anticipated future is showing up in the present. Helping their system face into the emerging future by using techniques such as scenario planning is one powerful way to help a system move within ever-changing times.

- *Belonging:* we all have a basic need to belong in a place where we can matter and feel secure, united within tacitly recognized webs of meaning — for example a team, department, nation, belief system, profession. In times of change, rituals and loyalties get disrupted and belonging can feel threatened. Effective leaders tune into these dynamics and pay attention to whether and how transition supports or threatens belonging.
- *Place:* any human system is an interconnected set of role relationships and competing hierarchies (is age or level more important here?) that are often disturbed in change — especially in restructurings. In ongoing change, lines of authority and accountability are fluid and might constantly shift and therefore require a leader's close attention. When place is unattended, people can be left feeling insecure and uncertain about their agency.
- *Exchange:* the universe is a vast system of exchange, every artery of it is in motion, throbbing with reciprocity. Good leaders tune into the 'give and the get' in any change where there will always be both beneficiaries and those who have to bear the price. By simply acknowledging any exchange imbalance (we once invited a team to stand in a line according to who had most to gain and most to lose) leaders can enable change to flow with greater ease.

Cultivating your inner state, paying attention to your outer action, taking care of how you design the change, and harnessing what governs a system's flow. Four potent and interconnected skill sets for leading in perpetual transformation. I wish you great Change Vitality in your future path.

About the author

Deborah Rowland is a pioneer thinker, practitioner, author and speaker in leading change. She has personally led change in major global organizations including Shell, Gucci Group, BBC Worldwide and PepsiCo, holding both Group HR and VP of Organizational and Management Development roles. Deborah is also the founder of consulting firm Still Moving which has pioneered research in the change field, and acts as change coach to the executive boards of major corporations. Her latest book, *The Still Moving Field Guide: Change Vitality at Your Fingertips* (Wiley, 2020) is based on her groundbreaking research into the realities of leading change.

Footnotes

104 https://iperceptive.com/authors/heraclitus_quotes.html

105 *Surfing the Edge of Chaos*, Pascale, R. (Currency, 2001)

106 *The Dance of Change*, Senge, P. et al (Nicholas Brealey, 1999)

107 *The Still Moving Field Guide: Change Vitality at Your Fingertips*, Rowland, D. (Wiley 2020)

108 *Leadership and the New Science*, Wheatley, M. (Read How You Want, 2012)

109 https://iperceptive.com/authors/heraclitus_quotes.html is this the right link?

110 *Still Moving: How to Lead Mindful Change*, Rowland, D. (Wiley 2018)

111 https://blogs.lse.ac.uk/businessreview/2019/02/07/lead-like-an-anthropologist-and-lead-change-well/

112 https://www.forbes.com/sites/sallypercy/2019/03/13/why-do-change-programs-fail/?sh=63755a342e48

113 https://blogs.lse.ac.uk/businessreview/2017/01/11/change-starts-with-a-leaders-ability-to-look-inward/

114 Man's Search For Meaning, Frankl, V (Rider, 2004)

115 https://wiki.santafe.edu/images/5/53/Lansing2003.pdf

116 https://medium.com/sfi-30-foundations-frontiers/emergence-a-unifying-theme-for-21st-century-science-4324ac0f951e

117 https://www.leadershipcentre.org.uk/artofchangemaking/theory/four-orders-and-constellations/

Eight implementation habits

ROBIN SPECULAND

20

Perpetual transformation requires organizations to have embedded eight key implementation habits.

Most of us start out with the right intentions when launching a new strategy, but somewhere between thought and action, we lose commitment. This happens for a number of reasons, such as being distracted by running the day-to-day business, or a new threat from the competition or geopolitical activities. Top performing organizations in perpetual transformation have embedded key implementation habits.

In the last few years, in strategy implementation, we have rapidly moved from acquiring *awareness* to needing *knowledge* to developing *behaviors*. This has been partly driven by the fact that the average strategy life cycle is now just three years, which means implementation is happening more frequently than ever before, and the skills to implement are more in demand.

Awareness in strategy implementation was ignited with a seminal *Fortune* article in June 1999, "Why CEOs Fail." Ram Charan and Geoff Colvin argued that the high strategy implementation failure rate was due to bad execution, not bad strategy. In 2002, they published *Execution: The Discipline of Getting Things Done*, and I published *Bricks to Bridges — Make Your Strategy Come Alive in 2004*. These books contributed to strategy implementation being recognized as its own field. (Note: "implementation" and "execution" are synonymous.) The books stressed that leaders need both the ability to craft the right strategy *and* the skill to implement it. In a 2015 HBR article[118] Leinwand, Mainardi and Kleiner revealed that, "Only 8% of Leaders Are Good at Both Strategy and Execution."

This massive gap between the ability to both craft and execute a strategy has evolved because leaders had been taught how to plan and not how to execute. The quest for knowledge about strategy implementation then saw a flurry of activity as leaders focused on improving the high rate of strategy implementation failures.

Today, strategy implementation has evolved and is focusing more on behavior. Leaders are now demanding consistency in the organization's ability to implement the strategy, what they call *perpetual* transformation. As Charan and Colvin said: "It's fascinating to watch what happens when a CEO who executes well brings these habits into a company where they didn't exist."

But, somewhere between planning the strategy and taking action to implement it, leaders typically lose their way. What is missing? The discipline to do what needs to be done and make implementation a positive habit.

It's critical in today's accelerated pace of business, with shortened strategy life cycles and the strain many leaders feel from turbulent markets, reduced working capital and board pressure to deliver right the first time. That's why implementation needs to become a habit.

Customers notice your implementation not your strategy

Much of the published literature to date still examines why implementation frequently fails rather than how to create a culture of perpetual transformation.

This article introduces, for the first time, eight implementation habits that have evolved from more than 20 years of research, client work and five books I've written on the topic. The habits are:

1. Discipline
2. Right Actions
3. Measure Everything
4. 90-day Chunks
5. Less is More
6. Nurture Communications
7. Culture of Accountability
8. Review Rhythm

Habit #1: Discipline

Implementation success requires ongoing discipline across an organization. There are no shortcuts. Discipline acts as the bridge across the turbulent sea of strategy implementation, propelling movement from thought to performance. As General H. Norman Schwarzkopf said: "The truth of the matter is that you always know the right thing to do. The hard part is doing it."

Embedding discipline is not easy. Consider that an estimated 40 percent of physicians are overweight and 44 percent of them smoke! Those paid to advocate healthy living don't appear to have the discipline to do what they know is right.

Changing strategy means changing how employees work. But getting them to do things differently does not result from a one-time town hall meeting announcing a new strategy. Rather, it requires leaders to provide constant daily support, reinforcement and encouragement to take new actions. Many leaders lack the discipline required to make this happen.

Like training for a marathon or becoming fit in the gym, action must become a daily discipline.

As a *rule of thumb,* adopt the discipline of practicing implementation habits by structuring it into the business. For example, I was working with a client in the Middle East, whose leadership team did not have the discipline to regularly review the implementation as they were always caught up with the day-to-day running of the business. To ensure the leaders adopted the discipline of regular reviews, so that they could take corrective action when required, the CEO established a separate leadership review meeting every two weeks. After eight months, this meeting was then absorbed into the regular leadership meeting as the leaders had adopted discipline of constantly reviewing and taking corrective action for the implementation of the strategy.

Review is just one of the eight areas required for excellence in execution.

Implementation Compass™

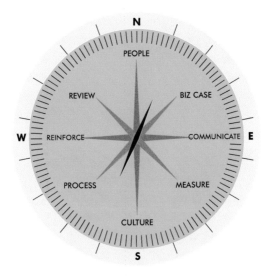

In *Bricks to Bridges — Make Your Strategy Come Alive,* I published the Implementation Compass™ — a framework of the eight areas required for excellence in execution. Organizations succeeding in their strategy implementation practiced these eight areas:

1) North: **People** — It's people who implement the strategy, not leaders. Leaders are responsible for ensuring the organization has the right caliber of people with the right skills.

(2) North-East: **Biz Case** — This explains *why* the organization must change strategies and create a sense of urgency around the required transformation.

(3) East: **Communication** — It's not only about creating initial fanfare but nurturing the communication by sharing customer feedback and informing employees what's going on, what's working, what's not working and what lessons are being learned.

(4) South-East: **Measurement** — A change in strategy requires a change in measurement. Leaders need to create the new measures that track the implementation and identify where to take corrective action.

(5) South: **Culture** — Culture drives the way the strategy is implemented. Two organizations can have the same strategy, but how they implement it is driven by their culture.

(6) South-West: **Process** — Processes need to be continually improved with employees empowered to change the way they are working.

(7) West: **Reinforce** — When employees step up and take the right actions, they have to be encouraged; otherwise, they will stop taking those right actions.

(8) North-West: **Regular Reviews** — Many leaders check on strategy implementation only once or twice a year. Frequent monitoring is critical as it reinforces the importance of the implementation and identifies where to take corrective action.

The Implementation Compass™ guides leaders through their implementation journey, identifying the right actions to take and drives the required discipline.

Habit #2: Right Actions

Changing your strategy, by default, means you're asking your employees to take different actions. Our research (Bridges Business Consultancy Int[119]) reveals that only 5 percent of employees know their organization strategy and only 12 percent of that group know the right actions to take.

Unfortunately too many strategy implementation launches do not clearly articulate to employees how the new strategy relates to them and specifically the right actions they can take to participate in the implementation.

With the launch of the new strategy, leaders are asking employees to do "more work," when many already have too much to do. The employees are already busy and now their leaders are asking them to do more! Leaders are responsible for encouraging and enabling employees to participate in the implementation and to make that participation as easy as possible.

One of the ways this can be achieved is to create a "To Stop" list. This identifies current actions in the organization that do not apply to the new strategy and need to be prevented. On the list, for example, might be eliminating old products or reports or a specific market segment.

The "To Stop" list creates the space, time and resources to focus on taking the right actions by eliminating non-value-adding actions.

My *rule of thumb* rule here is to come up with twice as many actions to stop as to start, so as to create the space to take the right actions. You will not always achieve this, but simply by aiming to do so assists in identifying actions to stop, as this is not a normal habit among leaders.

Once you have identified the right actions to take and eliminated the actions to stop, a powerful proven best practice is to allow employees to choose which of the right actions they want to take. This is because people are more committed to outcomes they set themselves by a ratio of almost five to one, as noted by Carolyn Aiken and Scott Keller of McKinsey.[120]

Aiken and Keller cite a famous behavioral experiment in which half the participants are randomly assigned a lottery ticket number while the others are asked to write down any number they want on a blank ticket. Just before drawing the winning number, the researchers offer to buy back the tickets from their holders. The result: no matter what geography or demographic environment, researchers found they had to pay at least five times more to those who came up with their own number. Why? Because people are more dedicated to outcomes they set themselves.

This can be put into practice by, for example, offering people a choice of which design thinking team they'd like to participate on. Ask: "Would you prefer to be on the design thinking team for onboarding new customers or one for improving the efficiency of our key product?"

The *rule of thumb* here is that small actions by lots of people equal big transformation. The aim for leaders is to explain and encourage employees to take the right actions.

Habit #3: Measure Everything

Measures drive the right actions, yet some leaders do not change their measures when they change their strategy. By default, they keep measuring the old strategy!

My *rule of thumb* here is: change your strategy, change your measures. Without the right measures in place:

- You won't know where you are along your implementation journey.
- You don't know which direction you are heading.
- People become confused when they're told one thing but measured against something else. When this occurs, they will continue to take actions based on achieving the old measures, not the new ones.
- You can't accurately show progress made from the baseline data to the targets.
- You don't know how your implementation is performing and therefore can't take corrective action.

A strategy scorecard is an exceptional tool for measuring and managing strategy and using it needs to become a habit in the organization. An effective strategy scorecard:

- Enhances leaders' understanding of the strategy across different business lines through discussions when the scorecard is created.
- Provides greater clarity about the strategy — what's important and what isn't.
- Allows leaders to speak with greater consistency in their messaging through a strategy story.
- Demonstrates both the importance of and commitment to the new strategy.

The following model I developed assists leaders in transitioning from vision to performance.

© Bridges Business Consultancy

The *vision* is the future state of the organization. The *mission* is its core purpose. The *values* are its guiding principles. The *strategy* is the detailed plan on differentiating yourself from your competitors and addressing how to achieve the vision. *Strategy objectives* further translate the strategy. Every strategy objective has at least one *measure*; every measure has an identified baseline and target attached to at least one action on how targets will be achieved. Individuals are held accountable for the *actions* they own. These actions are constantly reviewed to ensure the organization is on the right path toward the vision and delivering the expected *performance*.

It should be noted that of the eight areas highlighted in the above Implementation Compass, the area that receives the most resistance is "Measures." This is because poor performing organizations track employee performance once a year. With the introduction of a strategy scorecard leaders are able to track not annually, quarterly, monthly, or even weekly but daily. This creates a pushback from employees that can be the downfall of many and adoption of a strategy scorecard.

Habit #4: 90-day Chunks

In any transformation, early wins are required to build momentum and traction.

My *rule of thumb* here is to plan to take action in 90-day chunks. By consciously ensuring the actions can be completed within a 90-day period, leaders make the actions more manageable and they gain early traction.

180 days, for example, is too long as many people don't take the action until the day before they're about to be checked! 30 days is too short, as it leads to a list of too many actions to take. 90 days is just the right amount of time.

The motto is: "Theory promises and success sells." In this situation, the strategy is the theory, and the implementation is where success occurs by completing the right actions within 90 days. If more time is required, then the actions are divided into segments that can be completed within 90 days.

Habit #5: Less is More

Launching a strategy, as stated above means "more work" for employees, because they must continue running the current business while starting to implement the new strategy. Focusing on doing more, not less, has been the downfall of many strategy implementations.

When an organization launch has too many strategic objectives simultaneously, it can cause confusion about what's important, dilute resources and be detrimental to performance.

Carrefour's former CEO, Lars Olufsen, for example, took over the organization in 2009 and launched seven retail strategies including agility, customer engagement, innovation, and global expansion. What resulted from launching too many strategies simultaneously? Confusion across the organization, loss of domestic market share and a 53 percent plunge in share price in one year. Olufsen stepped down in 2012.

Compare this to Angela Ahrendts who joined Burberry as CEO in 2006. She announced five strategic priorities including intensifying non-apparel sales, accelerating retail-led growth and investing in underpenetrated markets. She stuck with these priorities for seven years, updating employees and investors regularly on progress against each goal. This reinforced the strategic message and the company's commitment to achieving those objectives. During this period, Burberry's share price handily outperformed competitors and the broader market.

My *rule of thumb* here is to focus on only three to five strategic initiatives within a 12-month period.

An experiment by Sheena S. Iyengar (Columbia University) and Mark R. Lepper (Stanford University) explains how less really is more.[121] They cite the Jam Experiment. It involved an upscale grocery store displaying, on one occasion, 24 jams for customers to view and purchase and, on the other occasion, only six different jams. Of the customers who visited the 24-jam selection, only 3 percent purchased. From the six-jam selection, 30 percent of the customers purchased — a 10-fold increase. This experiment also tested for choices of chocolate. Once again, the group being offered only six choices reported a higher level of satisfaction and made more sales than those offering more than six choices.

These conclusions indicate that leaders who promote three to five strategy objectives in 12 months realize greater achievements than those focused on many more. When organizations try to implement more than 10 objectives, less gets done and, in some cases, none of the objectives are completed.

When people feel overwhelmed, they do a little work on everything and finish nothing.

Habit #6: Nurture Communication

Every four years since 2000, my company, Bridges, has researched the state of strategy implementation.[122] In every research result, "poor communication" was among the top three reasons why strategy implementation fails. Even though leaders know communication is critical, they still lack the discipline to do it. For example, astonishingly, in many organizations, communication about the strategy is almost nonexistent six months after the launch. Communication often reverts to "business as usual," yet a wealth of communication needs to be shared, including:

- Progress against strategy objectives: This keeps employees informed on how the organization is performing.
- What's working and what's not: This creates a learning environment in which successes can be replicated and failures can be eliminated.
- Customer feedback: Listening to the voices of customers includes gathering their feedback on the strategy and sharing its implications.
- Progress against the metrics: This provides updates of the implementation analytics.
- Share success stories: This keeps employees engaged and encourages them to participate and take the right actions.
- Work improvements: This requires sharing how employees are changing the way they work.
- Milestones achieved: This celebrates successes.
- Strategy deviations: This explains any corrective action taken during the implementation and explains why.
- Lessons learned: This provides the opportunity for employees from different business verticals to share relevant experiences and lessons learned.

The *rule of thumb* here is to nurture communication throughout the whole implementation journey.

Habit #7: Culture of Accountability

When striving to achieve perpetual transformation, adopting accountability is essential. It requires holding someone responsible, with the emphasis on *one*. Leaders need to hold their direct reports regularly accountable, but they don't. This is frustrating as a culture of accountability is one of the easiest habits to adopt but one of the least practiced.

In Bob Proctor's book *It's Not About The Money*,[123] he notes how people who say, "that's a good idea" only had a 10 percent chance of making a change. Those who set a specific plan of how to do it had a 50 percent chance of making a change. But those who set a specific time to share their progress with someone else had a 95 percent chance of making a change. To set employees up for success with a 95 percent chance of making a change, take these six steps to help create a culture of accountability:

1. Know the organization's core values: The values act as guiding principles of what is important and acceptable.
2. Clarify expectations: People need to know how they're expected to perform and what they're expected to deliver *before* they can be held accountable. For example, does accountability mean attending meetings on time and/or submitting reports on time and/or checking that the right actions have been taken?
3. Adopt measures: Putting in place the right measures allows you to track performance, show what is important, and hold people accountable.
4. Assign one person: Don't have more than one person responsible because that eradicates the accountability.
5. Conduct reviews: People need to know they will regularly be asked how they did against the planned actions.
6. Link actions to consequences: People have to be recognized in a positive way when they take the right actions. There also needs to be negative consequences for inertia or the wrong actions, and the consequences must align with the values.

"The single most important change in actions that needs to occur during a time of cultural transition is the shift to greater accountability," say Roger Connors and Tom Smith in The Oz Principle.[124] And a survey of 161 companies by McKinsey & Company revealed that the number one best practice of agile organizations is role *clarity*, because it leads to greater accountability.[125]

The *rule of thumb* here is to let your employees know when you are going to hold them accountable and then do it.

Habit #8: Review Rhythm

Bridges' research[126] revealed that 85 percent of organizations spend less than 10 hours a month discussing their strategy implementation. In some organizations, it's only reviewed once or twice a year as leaders get distracted by other activities. When leaders become distracted from the strategy implementation, so do their people.

Successful implementation requires regular reviews. This establishes in the organization a review rhythm — a pattern and expectation that progress is checked. Leaders are responsible for conducting regular implementation reviews and making them a habit across the organization. How?

1. Every week, leaders ensure employees are asked by their immediate boss how they have contributed to the strategy implementation and identify where they need support and/or guidance.
2. Every two weeks, leaders review the strategy implementation performance within their own business vertical.
3. Every 12 weeks, the CEO conducts a quarterly review for the whole organization.
4. Every 52 weeks, leaders step back to reflect on the methodology and where it can be improved.

During the review , it is critical that the right questions are asked, for the answers will dramatically affect the actions taken by employees and the success of the implementation.

In *Atomic Habit*, James Clear wrote: "If you want to predict where you'll end up in life, all you have to do is follow the curve of tiny gains or tiny losses and see how your daily choices will compound 10 to 20 years down the line."[127] This is as true for organizations as it is for people.

To know where your organization could end up, ensure these eight implementation habits become a daily discipline on your journey to perpetual transformation.

About the author
Robin Speculand is a pioneer and expert in strategy and digital implementation. He is driven to transform strategy implementation globally by inspiring leaders to adopt a different mindset and approach. The founder of three organizations and three business associations, Robin is CEO of Bridges Business Consultancy Int and co-founder of the Strategy Implementation Institute and the Ticking Clock Guys. Robin is also a TEDx presenter and facilitator for IMD, Duke CE and Singapore Management University, and a prolific bestselling author. He recently authored *World's Best Bank: A Strategic Guide to Digital Transformation*.

Footnotes

118 https://hbr.org/2015/12/only-8-of-leaders-are-good-at-both-strategy-and-execution

119 www.bridgesconsultancy.com/research-case-study/research

120 www.mckinsey.com/business-functions/organization/our-insights/the-irrational-side-of-change-management

121 https://pubmed.ncbi.nlm.nih.gov/11138768/

122 www.bridgesconsultancy.com/research-case-study/research/

123 www.amazon.com/Its-Not-About-Money-Bob-Proctor-audiobook/dp/B001U5P7CA/ref=sr_1_1dchild=1&gclid=CjwKCAjwj8e JBhA5EiwAg3z0mwxm XGaYbny0Uuk4EMUmph VWAargtnL9I BYbM6T9AByP5A dqop6FpRo CaeYQAvD_BwE&keywords=it%27s+ not+ about +the+money+bob+proctor&qid=1630710323&sr=8-1

124 https://www.amazon.com/Oz-Principle-Individual-Organizational-Accountability-ebook /dp/B0012M2IX2

125 www.mckinsey.com/business-functions/organization/our-insights/the-five-trademarks-of-agile-organizations

126 www.bridgesconsultancy.com/research-case-study/research/

127 https://jamesclear.com/atomic-habits

Talking
transformation

BEHNAM TABRIZI

21

ehnam Tabrizi is a world-renowned expert and champion of
organizational and personal transformation. He has been teaching
Leading Organizational Transformation at Stanford University's
Department of Management Science and Engineering and executive
programs for more than 25 years. He is the author of six books,
including *Rapid Transformation* (HBR Press, 2007) for companies and
The Inside-Out Effect (Evolve Publishing, 2015) for leaders. He talks
perpetual transformation with Thinkers50 cofounder, Stuart Crainer.

*Stuart Crainer: One striking thing about you Behnam is that you not only
talk about and research transformation, but your life is actually a story of
successfully dealing with and living through transformation.*

Behnam Tabrizi: Yes, my life has been a series of perpetual transformation
and disruptions. I was born in Iran, and during the Iranian Revolution we had
to leave the country immediately. My mom worked at the U.S. Embassy. She
was teaching Farsi to the attaché and the ambassador. My dad was a Harvard
MBA with scholarship graduate. And so neither of them were really wanted
in the country, and their lives were in danger so we left very rapidly with an
empty suitcase.

We came to the U.S. and were on food stamps living in drug-infested
projects. And then I had to be the head of my family right after college, taking
care of my really young brother who was seven years old and my sister who
was 15 as well as my ill dad. So, there was a huge level of disruption.

*Stuart: For you, like so many others from immigrant families, education
was the way forward.*

Behnam: Yes, I studied computer science and then worked as a scientist at
IBM Research. Later I became tired of the technical world and went to Stanford
Business School. They were interested in people with a technology and science
background. My thesis was about prototyping. So I did a large-scale study of
the global computer industry, and in the early 1990s found that the more you
prototyped in uncertain environments, the faster you got to market and the
more successful you were likely to be. This was the research foundation for
design thinking and agile development.

I was doing well at Stanford. The advisor for my thesis was Kathy Eisenhardt. Then, in 2001, I had another disruption when I went through a complete spiritual breakdown. So I decided I wanted to have my life be about service. I made a goal of transforming the lives of 100 million people before I die. Since then I've been focused on transformation.

Stuart: And this work has brought you into contact with some great leadership figures.

Behnam: After my doctoral work, I trained 7,000 people at Intel and worked with Andy Grove. I also worked with Steve Jobs at NeXT during his hiatus from Apple. And then I had the privilege of working as an advisor on transformation with President Obama and Pope Francis. I'd been working with the Vatican on their transformation.

Stuart: And this led to your book Rapid Transformation?

Behnam: Yes, it was a large-scale study of transformations that led to counterintuitive results. Next, given my own personal experience and working with leaders, I realized the key to transformation is not just organizational transformation, but personal transformation. That's why I wrote the book on 2015 on the inside-out effect, which I'm really proud of. The marriage of psychology and sociology has helped a lot in terms of being able to really make a difference and coach companies.

Also, two years ago, I decided to partner with the Project Management Institute (PMI) because they have two million members and I wanted the work to be in front of as many people as possible.

Stuart: All the research suggests that companies are still very bad at achieving change. Something like 80 percent of change programs fail, but what you're talking about, transformation, is much more demanding and far reaching. So realistically only a small number of organizations are going to get anywhere near mastering it.

Behnam: Yes. To be a master, you can go from a white belt to a green belt, to a brown belt. It's a journey, a mountain with no top. Consultants love the linear change model because it takes four or five years. They can transform the supply chain, then marketing and so on. Just imagine how many billable hours that is! With my approach, basically you have a coach or two, you don't have an army of consultants. The people inside author the change. It's much more sustainable, and it moves rapidly.

Stuart: This has led to your most recent research into perpetual transformation.

Behnam: I have completed a deep, deep study of 22 organization — including Amazon, Apple, Netflix, Tesla, Haier, Intel, KBank in Thailand, Starbucks, Zara, and Santa Clara County. I have also looked at Blockbuster, Kodak and Nokia, among others, which failed to transform.

The starting point for those which succeed is what I call meta-agile leadership — meta means being able to zoom out, and agile is about pivoting and moving quickly. This is the antidote to organization stasis and mediocrity.

I found in all these successful organizations that they have controlled chaos. So from the outside while they look amazing, inside it's chaotic.

Stuart: One of the companies you feature in this research is the Chinese company Haier. It is a company I know well, and I'm always amazed by the level of ambiguity and chaos within the organization, and they're comfortable with that.

Behnam: The Chinese can handle ambiguity better than any Asian country, maybe better than anyone else in the world. So they're very comfortable with that chaos because in their DNA I feel the sense of entrepreneurship — something you can see at Haier.

Stuart: You also bring an existential understanding of what is actually going on in such organizations.

Behnam: From a meta point of view, what has really fascinated me in the past 10 years or more is why people are willing to die for a cause, but work for money? And that cause is what I am really interested in. The inside out effect is about having the personal compass. It's about a model where you can have meaning and also happiness and take advantage of all the strengths you have and be able to have that sweet spot in terms of your personal compass.

Microsoft has done this with every employee in the organization. In the military, the marines and special forces are amazing at this. KBank in Thailand has done it. Google has done quite a bit of this. Amazon is adopting this. There is this evangelism that exists in these successful companies that is just truly amazing. One of my favorite mentors at Stanford was Jim March. Jim pointed to Don Quixote as a great example of existentialism. He does not accept reality, but imposes his imagination, commitment and joy on it. This produces a life of beauty and meaning. I see a lot of that in successful organizations.

Stuart: So, a starting point is the organizational culture?

Behnam: Their organizational DNA is to see their work as life or death. That is what Andy Grove used to talk about, a feeling of paranoia. As one leader told me it's like piloting a plane and facing a mountain and trying to make a right angled turn. They always create a sense of life and death urgency. It feels like a cult, a religion. Think of Tesla or Amazon. These are not cults in the extremist sense — such cults disenfranchise people and people often cannot escape. Apple and other organizations bring the best of people out by connecting to who they are as an individuals.

Stuart: If that sort of commitment is the starting point what follows next?

Behnam: Tempo. There is an agility, a kinetic energy that the leaders bring in to increase the velocity. From a tempo point of view, there's also a meta part, which is the cadence. And the cadence is also very, very quick. Look at the Amazon-S team. It's the senior team, but also they bring in people and meet sometimes weekly. They talk about lots and lots of detail. HR is involved, finance is involved. They talk about big ideas. Everybody gets that tempo and the urgency. And they go several layers deep in Amazon, the six-page narrative — another way to create tempo — because when you put a six-page narrative together in meetings, people don't ask you a lot of questions that might show up in PowerPoint slides. They have read this and they have much more depth and much higher meta-temporal-type questions. The bottom line on tempo is that there's room in organizations to boost performance by ramping up pace. We have a lot of slack in companies. Leadership needs to take the slack and turn it into great results.

Stuart: Another aspect of this is the ability to combine exploitation and exploration. Can you tell me about that?

Behnam: What I realized at Intel was that it was great at exploitation. In fact, some of their ideas — such as on constructive conflict — are now being taught at Google, Amazon and Facebook. In my doctoral thesis, I talk about a bimodal approach to running an organization. One is what I call compression, which is about exploitation. And it's about really squeezing the steps, it's about moving things closer together — lots of parallel steps. And the other model was experiential, which is exploration, which has lots of iteration, powerful leaders and so forth.

Intel people did not have a lot of patience for exploration. But Amazon, Apple and Tesla do it really, really well. The mindset is long term. It's about experiments and failures. I love Jeff Bezos' personal motto — *Gradatim Ferociter* — step ferociously. It is stitched into his cowboy boots and is also the motto for his next Blue Origin venture. He argues that you cannot skip steps. Things take time. There are no shortcuts, but you want to do those steps with passion and ferocity. In every new business at Amazon, we see that.

Apple is the same. They take their time when they need to, and they move fast when they need to, especially when it relates to exploration. They're not into quick profit-making. At Tesla, you hear the word 'scrappy' all the time. They are never satisfied, always pushing back to improve things. These successful organizations are bimodal. For example, Amazon is religious about lowering costs, frugality and improving the customer experience.

Stuart: The organizations and leaders you talk about, from Andy Grove to Zhang Ruimin at Haier, are not really into comfort zones and status quo. But aren't they always fighting human nature?

Behnam: You're 100 percent correct. These are tough environments, but they also help you become the best version of yourself. It's a liberating experience. So while you're in it, it's crazy, but the number of wins you have, the things you learn, it's really accelerated learning.

Stuart: The language you use is completely different from the language which has been traditionally used about change. You're talking about existentialism, and the meta- and agile-led leadership, it's very different from the linear approach. So are you saying that the linear approach is dead?

Behnam: Yes. It was good for its time, but given the new reality, you really need this agile, rapid, concurrent transformation.

Stuart: The relationship between personal transformation and organizational transformation is an interesting one because in a company like Amazon, it is still very personal to Jeff Bezos, isn't it?

Behnam: People like Jeff Bezos are Pygmalion to organizational Galatea. That's the X factor. Pygmalion dedicated himself to his work and created Galatea, his sculpture. It's a beautiful statue of a woman, made with a lot of affection. Finally Aphrodite took pity on the young man, brought the statue to life, and they became lovers and lived happily ever after. So people like Bezos bring the best version of themselves in the organization. They also inculcate the seeds of their values into them. And to me, that is a liberating experience to be trained under Jeff Bezos, Tim Cook, Elon Musk, or Zhang Ruimin.

Stuart: What is also clear from your work is that all of this is based on an obsession with customers.

Behnam: Haier has thousands of microenterprises. Their guiding light is what they call zero distance between employees and customers. Likewise, Amazon, obsessively focus on the customer experience — selection, ease of use, low prices, more information. Zara is another great example. Or think of Steve Jobs: he encouraged all his people, all the experts, because Apple is a company of experts, to become experts in the field, to have their own experience and bring them in to produce products that customers could not even imagine. You don't want your customer to like you, you want them to love you. This is what customer obsession is.

Stuart: *Again, it has to come from the top.*

Behnam: One of my favorite movies is *Braveheart*. At some point in that movie Mel Gibson talks to the would-be king and the would-be king wants to play safe because he is worried about the likely reaction from his noblemen. He says, "Just remember, people don't follow titles, they follow courage." These leaders, whether it's Haier, Amazon, Apple, Tesla, have a lot of courage. Not only do they disrupt their business continuously, they also disrupt themselves. If you look at Steve Jobs' personal transformation from Apple 1 to Apple 2, it is night and day.

When Apple wanted to get into the retail business, I thought they're not going to be successful, because I was thinking about Gateway and other models. These guys are not like that. They think meta. They see this as a challenge. Think of Amazon with the Kindle. People told Bezos, Sony has tried it, so have others, and it didn't work.

Stuart: *What do you say to organizations when they say, well, what can we do tomorrow? What's the first step in this path?*

Behnam: Well, I would say starting tomorrow, let's get some of your best thought leaders and let's get out of our current environment. Let's just go somewhere. The CEO has to come and ask people what would you do if you were the CEO? What would you do differently? That sort of open conversation creates a sense of urgency. Openness is key as personal transformation needs to be aligned with where the organization goes. So we have to show vulnerability, we need to talk about our stories. We need to show a different face to each other, because we're going to go through choppy waters so we need to understand each other.

Once people melt their egos, we get them to talk about their environment and five to seven things that potentially could be a huge lever of change. It could be about the culture, but I've never been to a transformation that didn't have innovation. So we come up with seven bullet points and then we say, how do we engage the rest of the organization? This is the rapid track task formation thinking. How do you get your thought leaders to author a future so that they feel like it's their baby and not yours. Then we go a few layers down. We get these people together in a flat organization, we rapidly do a pre-transformation and in a period of about 90 days to 120 days, we come up with a blueprint for a major transformation and innovation in terms of culture and so forth.

We recognize there is a matrix in this organization, it's like a movie matrix, and we take people out of this matrix so that they feel like they matter, that the organization brings their best out. The best ideas are discussed to create a blueprint of the future. You change the culture outside of this matrix, and then you transpose it back to the organization. You have to be bold and courageous. Then I would also personally coach the CEO. Even CEOs have blind sides. You have to have their trust. They have to feel like they can open up to you, but you must identify their blindside and you've got to tell them if you don't change, if you're not willing to change, nothing is going to happen. So that also is a part of this whole process of perpetual transformation.